T0381303

THE SOUTH MISSISSIPPI CONFERENCE OF THE AFRICAN METHODIST EPISCOPAL ZION CHURCH

THE HISTORY, THE HERITAGE

HERITAGE EDITION

Compiled and Edited By Rev. Barbara Devine Russell

AuthorHouse™
1663 Liberty Drive
Bloomington, IN 47403
www.authorhouse.com
Phone: 1 (800) 839-8640

Published by AuthorHouse 04/25/2018

ISBN: 978-1-5462-2256-9 (sc)
ISBN: 978-1-5462-2257-6 (e)

THIS BOOK IS DEDICATED TO:

GOD WHO CREATED US

JESUS CHRIST WHO REDEEMED US

THE HOLY SPIRIT WHO GUIDES AND SUSTAINS US

IN HONOR OF BISHOP MILDRED B. HINES,
PRESIDING PRELATE, SOUTH MISSISSIPPI CONFERENCE
OF THE WESTERN DELTA EPISCOPAL DISTRICT
OF THE AFRICAN METHODIST EPISCOPAL ZION CHURCH

On behalf of the Conference Workers
Of the South Mississippi
Conference
Of the A.M.E. Zion Church

"O SEND FORTH THY LIGHT AND THY TRUTH, AND LET THEM GUIDE ME TO THY HOLY MOUNTAIN, AND LET THEM LEAD ME TO THE PLACE WHERE YOU LIVE.

Psalm 43:3

ALL HAIL THE POWER OF JESUS NAME
Edward Perronet and James Eller

All hail the power of Jesus Name,
Let angels prostrate fall
Bring forth the royal diadem,
And crown Him Lord of All.

Ye chosen seed of Israel's race,
Ye ransomed from the fall,
Hail Him who saved you by His grace,
And crown Him Lord of all.

Let every kindred, every tribe,
On this terrestrial ball
To Him all majesty ascribe
And crown Him Lord of All

Acknowledgements

I graciously extend thanks to God, our Lord and Savior Jesus Christ and the Holy Spirit for the inspiration, ability and resources to bring this project to fruition. I thank Bishop Mildred B. Hines for entrusting us with this assignment and for her support and encouragement given during this endeavor. I am appreciative to the Pastors for their assistance in submitting the histories in a timely manner. I truly thank the Conference Workers, Sallie Adams, Edna Pendelton and Stephanie Robinson for their contribution. Others who rendered technical assistance were Evelyn Mixon, Tasha Lewis, Joycette Nichols, Patricia Anderson, and Timberly Jones.

Special Thanks to Rev. Dr. John C. Evans, Jr., and the Cathedral Church Family for the use of their time and resources. I thank Ms. Earnestine Davis for her time and patience, for the writing and re-writings and the copies she provided on behalf of this project. The staff of the Canton Public Library, Ms. Maudell Evans, Ms. Tanesha Walker, Ms. Quinella Lewis and Mrs. Christine Greenwood, were very helpful with time, assistance and encouragement.

To Ms. Cynthia Goodloe Palmer, for creative assistance for the cover and layout design. To Ms. Sheila Summerall, of the Canton Vocational Technical Center, for editorial assistance. I am grateful for the church historians for their meticulous work in gathering the histories and submitting them in a timely manner and to Mrs. Hattie Chambers for meticulous critique on the overall document and a final reading. I am thankful to God and our Lord and Savior Jesus Christ for giving me the vision and the privilege to produce this sacred document for the posterity of the South Mississippi Conference. I pray that this work will continue perpetually, not only in the South Mississippi Conference, but throughout the African Methodist Episcopal Zion Church. TO GOD BE THE GLORY forever, and ever, amen..

INTRODUCTION

This book depicts the history of the establishment of the South Mississippi Conference and the growth and expansion of the churches that comprise the Conference from its inception to the present, which covers a period of approximately two hundred fourteen years. The history of these churches testify that the light of Zion Methodism dawned in the Southern-most part of the United States of America beginning with the west Tennessee and Mississippi Conference which was organized in October 1869, by Bishop J. J. Clinton, in Coffeeville, Mississippi. Rev. T. A. Hopkins, the first missionary to the State of Tennessee assisted Clinton. Reverends William Murphy, Grandison Simms, Alexander J. Coleman, Daniel J. Adams, I. J. Manson and L. J. Scurlock were the leading men in spreading the borders of Zion throughout Mississippi and West Tennessee. These men with others, expanded from this conference into Arkansas.

This was the beginning of the African Methodist Episcopal Zion Church in the South, Southwest and West. After Emancipation and the Civil War, the church continued to grow in its original territory and to spread into new territory

The South Mississippi Annual Conference was organized in December 1891 by Bishop Cicero Harris at Meridian, Mississippi as a result of a split from the West Tennessee Mississippi Conference. The Northern portion which extended from Memphis, Tennessee to Greenwood, Mississippi retained its original name, Tennessee and Mississippi Conference.

The Southern portion which extended from Yazoo City to Cookesville, Mississippi to Sherman, Alabama was named the South Mississippi Conference, each having two Presiding Elder Districts. (William J. Walls, "The African Methodist Episcopal Zion Church, Reality of the Black Church").

In a special Conference convened in December 2013, at St. Paul A.M.E. Zion Church in Canton, Mississippi, Bishop Mildred B. Hines, split the SMC into three Presiding Elder Districts, (Jackson-Gallman, Canton-Panola and Canton-Sharon), an historical move which was necessary to increase efficiency and stimulate growth in the SMC. Each District consists of eight churches.

We embarked upon this task with fear and trembling, desiring to honor God in every line, and to present an orderly account of our history for the generations to come; that they may appreciate and embrace the Heritage, develop a greater love and reverence for God, and the AME Church, and be faithful witnesses for Jesus Christ.

The task is a sacred one, worthy of the utmost attention and preciseness and determination to pass on the history of the churches as it was told to us by eye witnesses and those to whom the histories have been entrusted so that all can be assured of the accuracy and truthfulness of the writing. God is so worthy to be praised; and His mercy is everlasting and His truth endures to all generations.

We asked each church to provide us with a history of their church. We have been careful not to alter "one jot or one tittle" of that which was written by the respective church historians. It was noted that each church presented a history that was carefully and thoughtfully prepared, with a

Holy reverence for God, as the Holy Spirit gave the inspiration and the ability.

It is our sincere desire that this document will give us a better appreciation and love for our Heritage as the Freedom Church. We also hope that it will serve as an incentive for our youth that they will be motivated to live for and serve Jesus Christ, learn more about the AME Zion Church and appreciate our Christian Heritage as a liberated people who have been sent to liberate others through the propagation of the Gospel of Jesus Christ and through Christian Service to mankind.

PREFACE

"And the Lord answered me, and said, write the vision, and make it plain upon tables, that he may run that readeth it. For the vision is yet for an appointed time, but at the end it shall speak, and not lie: though it tarry, wait for it; because it will surely come, it will not tarry.
Habakkuk 2:2, 3

Prior to the Civil War, in the early 1800's, missionary activity was vigorous in the South. Missionary preachers were spreading the Gospel of Jesus Christ throughout this region, and societies were being established.

It was during the aftermath of the Civil War and Reconstruction, when the church was on the frontline of the battle, if it was to survive even the nation itself. In answer to the question asked by Sojourner Truth to Fredrick Douglass, "Fredrick, is God dead?" "No, he answered, "and because God is not dead, slavery can only end in blood". Sixteen years later, black men, slave or free, were being conscripted to fight in a Civil War that was to unite a nation torn apart by the men whose hearts had not been "strangely warmed" by the power of the Holy Spirit.

One can only imagine the destruction of life and property, the slaves who were discarded by their masters, those who escaped the wrath of those angry masters who vowed to not let them go, and the untold misery that was rampart throughout the slave states in the post-Civil-War days. The realization of what happened to the church in that period, twelve years of rebuilding that which was destroyed, the bringing together of displaced families, trying to adjust to this new found freedom proved to be fertile ground to resume missionary activity in the southern states. The African Methodist Episcopal Zion Church connection had been soundly established throughout the north, east and west.

The founding fathers were of African descent. Its preachers (missionaries), were imbued with the thirst for freedom, love for God and love for all of God's children. They pioneered in organizing prayer bands, and churches all over the south. They traveled on foot, in wagons, and by whatever means that were available during that time.

The A.M.E. Zion Church had held its sixth General Conference before 1847. While the convention was slowly but surely advancing the cause of freedom to worship and praise God unhampered by shackles of exclusion, the nation as a whole could not exist half free, half slave.

Three of Zion's most noble advocates and soldiers of the freedom cause, Fredrick Douglass, Harriet Tubman and Sojourner Truth were among those who set the nation aflame with their cry for freedom, "let my people go". After the Civil War, the late 1890's and the early 1900's ushered in new blood. Missionaries and ordained ministers from all parts of Zion joined in the struggle to build and rebuild that which has been destroyed by the ravages of war.

The period of reconstruction had brought about a more vigorous and powerful pronouncement of the new found freedom. God had wrought a mighty work for his people in Zion. As a free people we have purchased our own land, built our own houses of worship. Thanks be to God who has given us the Victory through our Lord and Savior, Jesus Christ.

In whom also we have obtained an inheritance, being predestinated according to the purpose of him who worketh all things after the counsel of his own will:

Ephesians 1:11

CONTENTS

HOLY, HOLY, HOLY

By: Reginald Heber

Holy, Holy, Holy, Lord God Almighty
Early in the morning, our song shall rise to Thee
Holy, Holy, Holy, merciful and mighty
God in three persons, blessed trinity

Holy, Holy, Holy, all the saints adore thee
Casting down their golden crowns around the glassy sea
Cherubim and seraphim, falling down before thee,
Which wert and art and evermore shall be

Holy, Holy, Holy, through the darkness hide thee
Through the eyes of sinful men thy glory may not see
Only thou art holy, there is none beside thee
Perfect in power, in love and purity

Holy, Holy, Holy, Lord God Almighty
All thy works shall praise thy name in earth and sky and sea
Holy, Holy, Holy, merciful and mighty,
God in three persons, blessed trinity

Chapter 1

The History of the African Methodist Episcopal Zion Church

The African Methodist Episcopal Zion Church was established in 1796, in New York City by James Varick, Abraham Thompson, William Miller and June Scott. The church was an outgrowth of the Methodist Episcopal Church, and was necessitated because of discrimination and denial of religious liberty in the kind of treatment they received in the services of the church.

Black preachers were prohibited from preaching, even to other Blacks except occasionally, and never among the Whites. They could not establish churches or missions in the field nor join the Annual Conference. They were assigned sections in the White churches marked "BM" meaning "Black Members". They were discriminated against in the administering of the Sacraments in that they could not receive Communion or Baptism until the Whites had been served.

After an incident occurred in which a minister was baptizing children, when he was finished baptizing the White children, he looked up in the gallery and said, "now you niggers can bring your children down." A sister brought her child and presented him. When the minister said, "name the child", the mother said, "George Washington". The minister looked at her for a moment as though she was guilty of some crime, and said "George Washington, indeed, his name is Caesar, Caesar", I baptize thee, etc."

After suffering many other indignities, this small group of restless, dissatisfied Christians, led by James Varick, Abraham Thompson, June Scott and William Miller, withdrew from the Methodist Episcopal Church and with wholehearted determination and zeal made the giant step in eliminating brutal slavery and proscription. From then on they moved with magnifying force, not only to produce some of the world's greatest freedom fighters and advocates, but went on to establish the first African Methodist Episcopal Zion Church, also known as the "Freedom Church." Spiritual, social, and economic emancipation were the hallmarks of their faith. It boasts as some of its members: Harriett Tubman, Frederick Douglas and Sojourner Truth, to name a few.

The organization now encompasses 3,000 churches and it has an active membership of 1.5 million members. The Church has founded and contributed to a number of institutions of higher learning.

Livingstone College with its affiliate, Hood Theological Seminary, Lomax Hannon Junior College in Alabama, Clinton Junior College in South Carolina; Dinwiddie Institute in Virginia; and African Methodist Episcopal Zion Junior College in Monrovia, Liberia, West Africa, and maintains missions here and abroad. The Star of Zion, the church's newspaper, is published biweekly.

The organization and structure of the church is discovered in the interpretation of its name:

AFRICAN: Denotes that the church would be led by the sons and daughters of Africa. The promotion of equality and parity among the human family would be their goal.

METHODIST: John and Charles Wesley, the founders of Methodism, emphasized the need for order and consistency in personal and public professions of faith.

EPISCOPAL: The denomination is supervised by Bishops who are elected by the General Conference. The jurisdictions of these Bishops comprise an international connection.

ZION: The term most frequently used in the Bible to describe the Church of God, Zion, was added to the name in 1848 to distinguish this demonization from other African Methodist bodies.

At present, the A.M.E. Zion Church is operative on five continents.

WHAT IS A METHODIST?

Methodism as defined by the founders, John and Charles Wesley, as a system whereby one lives according to the methods laid down in the Bible and is displayed by serious deportment and methodical habits of study and life.

The fundamental qualities of Methodism are characteristically expressed in the twenty-five Articles of Faith of the Methodist Religion. The expression of that "strange warming of the heart," which led to its beginning in a prayer meeting on Aldersgate Street, in London, May 24, 1738, when John Wesley learned what the Apostle Paul had discovered, that it is not by rules and laws; not by our own efforts at self-perfection; but by faith in God's mercy as it comes to us in Christ Jesus, that man may enter upon life and peace.

They believed the conversion should be manifested in a religion of individual experience, colored strongly by emotion and feeling, stressing an inward transforming, religious experience through Christ Jesus.

CHRISTIANITY AND METHODISM

The principles of Christianity are based upon the belief of a Universal God and the Brotherhood of man. The Christian religion has also boldly sponsored and defended freedom (barring its corruption) for all men. Christianity is the major thing the African American got out of slavery, second to which was the English language.

Methodism was embraced by the founding fathers because of John and Charles Wesley's strong opposition to human bondage, which made a noticeable impact upon the Negro population in the United States and West Indies during the late eighteenth and early nineteenth Century. Their attitude created an atmosphere in Methodism that went all through America to the emancipation of her slaves; and is still inherent in the freedom cause. John Wesley spoke almost with his dying breath when he declared, "American slavery, the vilest that ever saw the sun."

THE RESULT OF CHRISTIANITY ON THE AFRICAN AMERICAN

Christianity was first introduced to the African, African American, as a mechanism for exploitation and slavery, and for the slave trade. But what Satan meant for evil, God meant it for our good.

Christianity has been the single most important agent in the liberation and preservation of the African American race and heritage. History has recorded that some of the foremost abolitionist and advocates for human and civil liberties have been of the Christian faith, and, Zionites: namely, Frederick Douglas, Harriett Tubman and Sojourner Truth.

The South Mississippi Conference
Of the
The African Methodist Episcopal Zion Church
Southwestern Delta Episcopal District
Bishop Mildred B. Hines, Presiding Prelate
Mrs. Gwendolyn Brumfield, Missionary Supervisor

Quadrennial Theme:

Exhibiting God's Worth
Through our Praise, Worship, Discipleship and Stewardship

Quadrennial Motto:

ExPect

The

Great

THE HERITAGE EDITION IS PROUD TO INTRODUCE THE 98TH BISHOP IN SUCCESSION OF THE A.M.E. ZION CHURCH

The Southwestern Delta Region of the African Methodist Episcopal Zion Church spans the following states

OKLAHOMA
ARKANSAS
TENNESSEE
TEXAS
LOUISIANA
MISSISSIPPI

Members of "Hines Team" accompany her to the Mid-Winter Board of Bishops'
Meeting, December 2013, held in Houston, Texas, at which she presided
(Lt.- R. fr row): Rev. Bessie Martin, Rev. Lelar Brooks, Rev. Dr. Floyd E. Chambers, Bishop
Mildred Hines, Rev. Dr. John C. Evans, Jr. Rev. Gary D. Adams, Sr. Rev. Yolanda Lowe.
(Center): Ms. Camille Brown, Ms. Betty Nichols, Rev. Isabel Scott, Jackie Thompson, Sis.
Heidi Jones and Harris Ruth Brown: Rear: Rev. Dr. Peggy McKenny, Rev. Acquanette Johnson,
Sis. Linda Luckett, Ms. Sallie Adams, Rev. Ola Dixon, and Rev. Bonnie Travis.

At the 123rd Session of the South Mississippi Conference, December 2013, Bishop Hines made sweeping changes. In addition to creating a third Presiding Elder District, Bishop shared with the conference that she is an avid sports fan and her sport of choice is track, at which she was pretty good in her school days. Sometimes while ministering, and in the spirit, she might get the desire to "leap" over the pulpit. It was in this spirit that the "Team Hines" spirit was introduced and embraced in the SMC. It is also understood that the "**Team Hines** Spirit is driven by the determination to **do it right**". It is a spirit of being attentive to every detail and being thorough in every encounter. "Team Hines" adopted the official Motto: "EXPECT THE GREAT" for this conference quadrennial.

Let the Elders that rule well be counted worthy of double honor, especially those that labor in the Word and in Doctrine."

Chapter III

PRESIDING ELDER DISTRICTS

Canton
Sharon Rev.
Dr. John C.
Evans, Jr.

St. Paul-Canton
Greater Sims
Owens Chapel
Free Chapel
Sharon Chapel
Lees Chapel
Sharpsburg
Jerusalem Temple

Canton Panola
Rev. Dr. Floyd
E. Chambers

Greater Salem
Zion Chapel
Greater Murphy
Greater Middleton
Grove
St. Peter
Liberty
Hill
Walker Chapel
St. Paul-Cooksville

Jackson/
Gallman
Rev. Gary D.
Adams, Sr.

Cathedral
Greater Blair Street
Tabernacle of Grace
Gallman Chapel
Zion Hill
St. James
Free Union
Victory

THE JACKSON-GALLMAN DISTRICT

The Jackson-Gallman District is spearheaded by Rev. Gary D. Adams, Sr., the Pastor of Zion Chapel A.M.E. Zion Church.

Rev. Adams is a respected leader and outstanding teacher in the South Missisippi Comference. He is the Founder of Victory A.M.E. Zion Church on Cooper Road, Jackson, Mississippi, and was the first pastor of that church.

Previous churches he has shephered are, Free Chapel, Greater Blair Street, Salem and St. Paul, Canton, Mississippis.

He was appointed presiding elder of the Meridian-Kosciusko District in 2008 by Bishop Darryl B. Starnes and served in that capacity for four years. In the December 2012-2013 Annual Conference he was reappointed by Bishop Mildred B. Hines over the Meridian-Kosciusko District. In a special conference held December 2013, a third presiding district was created by Bishop Hines, the Jackson-Gallman District, and Rev. Adams was appointed Presiding Elder.

Rev. Adams is married to Mrs. Janeith Wilson Adams and they are the proud parents of three children, Denetria, Alicia and Gary, Jr., and two granddaughters, Madison and Kennedy.

CHURCHES OF THE JACKSON-GALLMAN DISTRICT

Cathedral
Greater Blair
Tabernacle of Grace
Victory
Gallman Chapel
Zion Hill
St. James
Free Union

EXPECT THE GREAT

CATHEDRAL AME ZION CHURCH – 1989-2013
A Church Making a Difference
Pastor: Rev. Dr. John C. Evans, Jr.

In 1989, Blair Metropolitan AME Zion Church was established by Rev. Dr. John C. Evans, Jr., Because of unprecedented growth and the necessity for a larger facility. Dr. Evans and members of Greater Blair Street AME Zion Church split from Greater Blair Street, leaving about 100 members at Greater Blair Street, and purchased a facility on Northside Drive, organized a society and named it Blair Metropolitan AME Zion Church.

Pioneers such as: Brothers Robert Singleton Chairman of the Board of Trustees, Arthur Levy; Frank Wilkerson; Virgil Robertson; Clarence Jefferson; Janie Easley, and many others gave their unselfish support to the pastor to secure the vision.

As the Lord allowed, many of the elders decided to remain at Greater Blair Street, and the Bishop appointed Rev. Gary Adams as its pastor. Today the church still remains as the Mother Church in Jackson.

Under Pastor Evans' administration, Blair Metropolitan continued to spiral upward. A daycare center was established, a library, bookstore, and a tutorial lab. During the early years at Blair Metropolitan, membership again tripled; Bible class increased, therefore, increasing its study times to Tuesday and Wednesday. The Sunday School Department grew to nearly 500 in attendance. Its superintendent, Grace R. George Walker, was used by God to develop a Sunday School Second to none. Also, a television and radio ministry was started and aired on WAPT Television and WOAD Radio.

As the church continued to grow and prosper, the need arose to alleviate two Zion Churches in the city with the name of "Blair." Blair Metropolitan changed its name to Cathedral A.M.E. Zion Church.

Through the years, a new parking lot was added and other needed renovations were made.

The ministry also became active in community affairs. Several apartment properties were acquired and named Exodus Ministries to provide low-income housing and a transportation building was purchased. The North Jackson YMCA was purchased and renamed Cathedral Activity Center. This facility now serves as a community service center where family and friends gather, and summer camp for children is held.

Later in 2003, an after school program was added to the facility to provide a safe and economical place for parents to send their children to an excellent after school program to assist with homework and other learning activities.

In October, 2013, Cathedral was blessed and favored by the Lord to burn its mortgage.

Cathedral A.M.E. Zion Church is continuing in the growth process. More than ever, Cathedral is seeking God's face and the leading of the Holy Spirit to walk into the "greater" He has for us and the "greater work" He has for us to do.

FREE UNION AME ZION CHURCH – 1875-2013
The Church that's "Small in Members, but Big at Heart".
PASTOR: Rev. Octavia Berry

Pastor Octavia Berry, being a daughter of Blair Metropolitan A.M.E. Zion Church under the pastorate of Rev. Dr. John C. Evans, Jr., was appointed the charge of Free Union in 1995 by Bishop Joseph Johnson, and has been the shepherdess of this little flock ever since.

She is described by members of Free Union as a sharing and courageous leader.

Free Union has undergone many transitions under pastor Berry's leadership. The original Free Union was gutted by a fire that destroyed the building in 2005. The congregation worshipped at Pickens Community Center for two years prior to purchasing Sacred Heart's church that became available when they built a new edifice.

Pastor Berry, boasts proudly that Free Union's children were the most knowledgeable Bible Scholars she has encountered in Zion. She says that Free Union's children were some of the most well educated in Zion, and boasts that many have achieved significant accomplishments in the field of education, law, and the military. Pastor Berry believes this is due to the excellent Christian education they received at Free Union.

(Free Union's History from inception to 1996 by: Rev. G.L. Johnson, former pastor)

May God's Eternal love forever bless the Free Union A.M.E. Zion Church and community. Glory be to God, and praises to His Son, Jesus Christ, for inspiring this endeavor of writing the history of Free Union A.M.E. Zion Church. This endeavor is the first of its' kind, but nonetheless, much needed in order to view the past, access the present and plan for the future.

Free Union A.M.E. Zion Church, Yesterday, Today and Tomorrow:

In light of this historical landmark, Free Union A.M.E. Zion Church, is just one of the thousands of churches that make up the Great A.M.E Zion Connectional Church.

Therefore, as we attempt to share with you the "Yesterday, the Today, and the Tomorrow of Free Union A.M.E. Zion Church, it is fitting and proper that we pause here and thank God for His Grace, Mercy, Wisdom, Understanding and Knowledge He imparted to our founding Fathers in their efforts to praise His Name. And, it is at this point we find ourselves giving God the praise and glory for lifting up the minds and hearts of our Founding Fathers of Free Union Church in 1875, when, according to the deeds filed in the Madison County Court House in Canton, Mississippi, that show Washington Ousley deeded to Scippero Fleming, William Green and Ben Ousley, the First Trustees of Free Union.

Again, we want to make it clear that this is the first attempt, to our knowledge of any other endeavor to write the history of Free Union. And because of this fact, we are without many written facts about the church. Therefore, we must serve upon the minds of our elder members to set forth as accurate record as possible, the true account of Free Union Church.

However, we feel the importance of commemorating the legacy of our Founding Fathers and recording the history and a written document of their activities and labors for God and our Lord and Savior Jesus Christ. Any mistakes made on our behalf, as the saying goes, "charge it to our head and not to our heart."

There can be no greater act on the behalf of mankind, than to establish a House of Prayer for the worship of God.

History serves us well that sin itself has intensified to the downfall of the human race, and to say the least, many people have been mistreated.

The A.M.E. Zion Church was born out of the desire on the part of African Americans to serve God without the cruelty of slavery, or the sin of white Americans that gave rise to the African Methodist Episcopal Zion Church in America. The very act of our Founding Fathers to say "NO" to their white brothers in the church, no doubt, displayed great courage, will-power, and steadfast faith in God. History will never let us forget that to be black in America during the evil days of slavery was outright dangerous.

Therefore, it is imperative that we preserve our church history and never forget God's goodness and love that He showed us by granting our Fathers courage to take a stand against slavery. As I read the deed of Free Union Church, I viewed the "X" mark made by brother Washington Ousley and took for granted that he was a black man.

Keeping in mind that education was not afforded our people, but realizing that the Spirit of God moved upon the hearts of His children to lift the shackles of slavery through worship.

The wood frame building that was situated in the NE ¼ of NE ¼ and E ½ of SE ¼ of NE¼ of Section Thirty (30) Township, Twelve (12) Range, 4 Est., or as I would describe this area from my childhood days, "Up in the red Clay Hills of Pickens," became known as Free Union A.M.E. Zion Church.

The Mississippi Conference of the A.M.E. Zion Church was organized in 1869 by Bishop J. J. Clinton, and not many years afterward, in 1875 Free Union was organized, becoming a part of the A.M.E. Zion Connection.

It was believed that around 1900, T. Fulton, Willie Green, Ben Ousley, Frank Mackey, Ned Gallaway, Dave Bolden, Mose Fleming, Scippiro Westbrooke, and their families, and others of the Free Union Community, moved the small wood frame Church to its present location. The land where the church presently sits is believed to have been given to the members. God motivated our forefathers to establish Free Union, and on August 4, 1919, T. H. Fulton and Vine Fulton deeded Trustees and their successors of the Free Union School, the land south of the lot owned by the A.M.E. Zion Church. This parcel of land also located in Madison County, Mississippi, was to be used for Free Union School. Although Free Union School did not survive, as did the Church, it must be remembered that many children received their formal education at Free Union School.

Free Union is a historical landmark that must be preserved for generations to come. With the founding of Free Union right after the Emancipation Proclamation by President Abraham Lincoln in 1863, it is our belief that the name "Free Union" was then, and is now, and will forever be the expression of Freemen to God Almighty for His Bountiful Grace and Love shown for His people.

Free Union A.M.E. Zion Church today, 1987, is blessed, first of all to have survived these one hundred twelve years, from 1875 to 1987. However, God has poured His love upon the church in so many ways.

First and foremost, the members are God-fearing people and possess a strong love of Jesus Christ in their lives. Simply put, the members of Free Union love one another. Also, Free Union A.M.E. Zion Church is blessed to have as its' Episcopal Leader, the Right Rev. Reuben L. Speaks, and the most gracious Episcopal Supervisor, his lovely wife, Jamie Speaks. Praise be to God for His continual blessing upon the A.M.E. Zion Church with such great leaders.

And still, too, Free Union is blessed to have as our Presiding Elder, Rev. Jimmie C. Hicks and his lovely wife, Eunice Hicks. I believe it is the general consensus of the Canton-Jackson District of the South Mississippi Conference that Rev. Hicks and his family have provided great Christian Leadership for many years. Let us be mindful of their Christian Education motto: "Learning to Do It Right." May God bless and keep our leaders in their efforts to be servants for the King, our Lord and Savior Jesus Christ.

The Tomorrow for Free Union A.M.E. Zion Church must reflect the yesterday, in that our founding fathers tasted the joy of freedom by saying to God, thank You for Free Union A.M.E. Zion Church. We must imagine in our heart what this meant to them, and work hard to make sure that there will always be a Free Union A.M.E. Zion Church.

We at Free Union A.M.E. Zion Church are aware that change is a way of life, but we are also aware that the wrong kind of change is no good for God's people, and in many ways the changes have caused men to forget the

One responsible for our freedom. Just the other Sunday, in Sunday school at Free Union, one of the Mothers of the Church said, "We don't love like we once did." How true, and without love, we cannot exist as God's people.

Therefore, "Tomorrow" at Free Union A.M.E. Zion Church is Jesus in our hearts".

Former Pastors at Free Union: Rev. Annie Tolbert, Rev. J.P. Phillips, Rev. Valerie Smith, Rev .Novie Chaney and Rev. G.L. Johnson.

Presiding Elders: Rev. John C. Evans, Jr. and Rev. Jimmie C. Hicks. Trustees: Brothers Edward Lindsey and Stasher, and Sister Sheila Cole.

Free Union, Free Union
That's the name we know;
Free Union, Free Union,
On and On we must go."

"Free Union A.M.E. Zion Church, Yesterday, Today and Tomorrow"

Historians: Rev. Octavia Berry and Rev. G. L. Johnson. (Rev. G. L. Johnson submits this historical account in memory of his mother, Mrs. Precious Rimmer, who raised him up in Free Union Church, and all the wonderful members of Free Union).

GREATER BLAIR STREET AME ZION CHURCH
1909-2013
"The Church Where Everybody is Somebody"
PASTOR: Rev. Rosie Jackson

Greater Blair Street A.M.E. Zion Church located at 1106 North Blair Street, Jackson, Mississippi, was founded by the late Rev. Fulford (first name not known), in early 1909. Being firmly rooted in his belief and evidently a man of vision, he united with the Pearl Street A.M.E. Church in order to be active in the body of Christ.

In 1909, Rev. Fulford organized a church mission in Hunts Hall on North Farish Street where the weekly rent was two dollars and fifty cents. Having begun without any adult members, God moved in a mighty way and twelve adults were added to the church. Meanwhile, the church was composed of children and young adults from the neighborhood churches.

One of the youth, Myra Moore, later became the wife of Rev. Fulford. Other pioneers were Sam Williams, Phil Bryant, Sam Brown, Daisy Brown, David Grady and Will Loft.

Mrs. Myra Moore Fulford was the first pianist. She and her husband were the first to receive scholarships for secondary training under the leadership of Dr. John Alstork, who was bishop at that time.

In the same your of 1909, Rev. Fulford purchased and donated to the church the lot on which he built the first church, and still is the present site of Greater Blair Street A.M.E. Zion Church.

The first Annual Cornerstone Ceremony was held in 1910, and in 1912, the first Annual Conference was held at Blair Street A.M.E. Zion Church. The following years were ones that brought hardships, but under the leadership of outstanding ministers such as Reverends D. S. Williams, McMullen, Blakeley and the Beards; all held fast to their dream.

However, disaster came and the church was blown down, but Rev. and Mrs. Beard kept the church alive by conducting services in a tent and later Rev. Blakeley was successful in increasing the membership.

Under the leadership of Reverend and Mrs. Beard and Rev. Blakeley, Blair Street owned its first parsonage. There were times when the church was unable to pay the pastor's salary, so the members would get together and "pound" the preacher. This means that members brought a pound of potatoes, meat, rice, etc. in order for the pastor and his family to survive. Being a man of God, Rev. Blakeley remained with the church and worked faithfully until he was assigned to another church.

In the early 1940's, Rev. G. W. Staffney came to Blair Street A.M.E. Zion Church. A man with his preaching ability and anointing was needed to restore and revive the church. By his forceful, soulful, preaching and inspirational singing, God was able to move mightily and nine hundred souls were added to the church. This was a miracle happening in the city. Here in the early 1940's a mega church was born.

After many transformations, trials, and hardships, the membership decreased, but in 1952, God had another ram in the bush. Rev. Novie S. Chaney, Sr., was appointed to Blair Street A.M.E. Zion Church. God inspired him and enabled him with a successful ministry. He built the first story structure which housed a sanctuary, business office, kitchen, dining room, educational area, and rest room for both men and women. Under his leadership, a parsonage was purchased, and he hosted a radio broadcast on radio Station WOKJ. This was the first for Zion

Church in Jackson. Many souls were added to the church and he planted a seed in the hearts of the people to build a new and modern edifice. He also married a daughter of the congregation, Odell Cotton.

In 1958, Blair Street again turned the page of a new exciting and dynamic life of the church. Rev. Raymond M. and Ellen Richmond were sent to pastor the church. It was under this leadership that the church name changed to the Greater Blair Street A.M.E. Zion Church. Rev. Richmond picked up the torch carried by Rev. Chaney and built a second story to the church's existing structure.

The church was further developed and added several needed ministries, the Class Leader System was implemented, the Chancellor and Gospel Choir were added, and eleven Sunday School Teachers volunteered their services. The church met the challenge of increasing its youth membership through implementing the Varick Christian Endeavor Society, VCE, and the Buds of Promise. Major ministries included the Birthday Club, Do-Something-About-It-Club and Sisterhood Ministries. These Ministries laid a lasting foundation for many of the ministries operating today.

Mrs. Ellen Richmond was the first person to hold a national position from our Episcopal area. She served as Superintendent of the Buds of Promise for eight years. Rev. Richmond served as Pastor of Greater Blair Street for twenty-one years. His son Raymond Richmond, Jr. continued to serve in the South Mississippi Conference as Conference Treasurer and Conference President of the Lay Council for many years after his parents were assigned to pastor in Tuskegee, Alabama.

In 1979, a son of the soil, Rev. Willie J. Neal, became Pastor of Greater Blair Street. He along with his wife, Janice Kenny Neal, A daughter of the house, continued the legacy of success in Zion. This pastoral team implemented a Bus Ministry and renovated the first story of the church structure, which included the installation of an elevator to assist the elderly. He reorganized the young adults and changed the choir name to the Holy Ghost Singers. He exclaimed that a name like that should inspire Holy Living. Also a junior choir was founded. Mrs. Neal took heart in teaching and training all children in the Junior Choir. She also introduced a speech choir, which encouraged many to speak distinctly and fluently.

In 1986, Rev. Ruben L. Speaks, Presiding Bishop of the South Mississippi Annual Conference of the African Methodist Episcopal Zion Church appointed a young man, age twenty-six, as pastor. Rev. John C. Evans, Jr., became pastor when the church was under attended, and sometimes lacked motivation for the things of God.

His anointing, motivation, energy and his steadfastness to stand on the Word of God, moved the church spiritually to a place unimaginable and incomprehensible to the congregation. His first order of business was to introduce the Holy Spirit as vital, necessary and crucial to the Christian walk.

With his love for God, preaching an uncompromising Gospel, and introducing a non-traditional worship service, the congregation experienced unprecedented growth both numerically and financially, necessitating a larger and more accommodating facility. Greater Blair Street travailed in labor. Pastor Evans and some of the members ventured out by faith and purchased a property on Northside Drive, Jackson, Mississippi, and Blair Metropolitan A.M.E. Zion Church was born.

Greater Blair Street A.M.E. Zion Church was reorganized in October 1989, resulting from the birth and purchase of Blair Metropolitan A.M.E. Zion Church. Approximately one hundred members remained at Greater Blair Street and held Sunday School for one Sunday after which its new owner, Ridgecrest Baptist Church claimed the church.

Presiding Elder, Jimmie C. Hicks met with the congregation for the purpose of future directions and reorganization. Brother Johnnie L. Cotton, Jr., was designated to serve as Lay Leader until a pastor was assigned.

The members were determined to remain a church, thereby holding meetings at various homes and sometimes at restaurants. Various committees were created as well as captains and contact persons for spiritual, moral and financial needs. It was suggested by Sis. Mary L. Simpson that each family pay $1,000.00 toward the first building fund in order to reclaim our church building. We collected a total of $8,000 in only two months.

In November 1989, Bishop Alfred L. White and his cabinet met with members at Grove Park to give directions for our future. Upon request, Rev. Willie J. Neal was assigned to us as our new pastor. We rejoiced because our prayers were answered.

Our first service as pastor and members was held at Jordan Grove M. B. Church in December 1990. In January 1991, we relocated to Bethlehem Center and in September 1991, with joy, praise, and thanksgiving, we returned to Greater Blair Street A.M.E. Zion Church. We thank God for all the souls who came to Christ since that time.

We also thank God for our first pastor, Rev. Willie J. Neal whose first message to us was "Everybody is Somebody in Jesus Christ." This was adopted as our church motto today and forever.

Rev. Gary Adams and his family came to us from November 1995 until November 1997. On April 17, 1996, a devastating fire completely destroyed the church sanctuary with minor damage to the lower level. As a result of this painful loss, we worshipped at People's Funeral Home. Following repairs to the lower level, we returned and held services until the sanctuary was restored.

Rev. Charles Darden was assigned to us in November 1997 and remained until November 1998. Bro. Andre Thames served as associate pastor.

The pews for the sanctuary were purchased under Rev. Gary Adams' administration, but were not delivered and installed until 1998. A new piano was donated on behalf of Sis. Lula Coleman by Mr. W. Wells and his son, Rev. Anthony Wells. We praised God and rejoiced for the opportunity to worship in the new sanctuary.

Rev. Fred L. Brown was assigned to Greater Blair Street in November 1998, as shepherd of the flock, and he remained until October 2003.

Rev. Arthur L. Davis and his family were assigned to Greater Blair Street A.M.E. Zion Church in October 2003. Under his leadership, souls were added to the church and a much needed van was purchased.

On February 4, 2007, our first female pastor, Rev. Dr. Belinda J. Johnson was assigned to Greater Blair Street. Under her leadership, souls were added to the church and a much needed van was purchased.

On December 23, 2012, Rev. Rosie Jackson, (picture above) was assigned by Bishop Mildred B. Hines. We look forward to great things with Rev. Jackson as our Spiritual Leader.

Since September 1990, we have weathered many storms, encountered sickness, death and troubled times. But by the Grace of God and the dedication and support of members and friends, we rejoice with thanksgiving that God will be glorified in all we say and do. Greater Blair Street A.M.E. Zion Church is truly a light from God for this community, city and state. As we move forward, through God's grace and mercy, we will continue to focus on Him and His will for this church.

With God as our guide, and Pastor Jackson as our leader, we will continue to move upward. We praise Him and bless His Name to day and forever!!!!!

Greater Blair Street Buds take the banner.
(rear-right) Rev. N.J. Neal, Pastor

TABERNACLE OF GRACE A.M.E. ZION CHURCH
1996-2013
"The Church that Thrives on Love"
PASTOR: Rev. Lillie Robinson

Tabernacle of Grace A.M.E. Zion Church was established in 1996 by Rev. Bessie Martin. Tabernacle of Grace is located at 800 Neal Street, in Clinton, Mississippi. Under the leadership of Rev. Bessie Martin, many souls were saved, delivered and filled with the Holy Spirit.

Renovations were done at the church with the addition of a fellowship hall and kitchen. A van was also purchased to transport members and/or future converts. After twelve years at Tabernacle of Grace, Rev. Bessie Martin stated that the Lord was leading her to leave Tabernacle for a work elsewhere.

The next pastor to carry the torch and lead the people was Rev. Roderick Briggs. He impacted the neighborhood by preaching and teaching the truth of the Word in power and demonstration. Rev. Roderick Briggs was appointed Pastor of Victory A.M.E. Zion Church and Rev. Quinton Hicks was appointed and performed duties of pastor from January 2009 until the first of April 2009.

Under the leadership of Pastor Lillie Robinson an extensive amount of remodeling has taken place so that the church could be safe to worship and a clean and nice environment that is conducive to praise and worship.

Rev. Bessie Martin and Home Mission of the South Mississippi Conference were so helpful in providing funds for most of the repairs, especially the roof. The members of Tabernacle and our families and friends made many financial sacrifices to help the church become what it is today.

God has been so good to us. Many souls are being saved, delivered and filled with the Holy Spirit and encouraged daily.

In the words of Rev. Bessie Martin, founder and first pastor of Tabernacle of Grace A.M.E. Zion Church, "In 1991, God gave me a vision to start a church beginning with a Bible Study. The Spirit said, this Bible Study would develop into a church. He revealed to me a building with a very high front constructed from the ground up. This church was filled with people from wall to wall and would operate in the five-fold ministry.

In May of 1993, after completion of Bible School from Word of Life, I contacted three young men from Blair Metropolitan under the leadership of Rev. John C. Evans, Jr., Calvin Dean, Tony Nicholas and Henry Garrett. These young believers assisted me in passing out flyers in the surrounding communities.

On Tuesday, January 11, 1994, I arrived at 6:45 P.M. at 800 Neal Street, Clinton, Mississippi in the Agape Community Center for the first Tuesday night Bible Study. The meeting was scheduled to start at 7:00 p.m. and four (4) people were waiting upon my arrival. I gave them a brief history of the vision the Lord had given me. The Bible Study opened with a praise song and prayer.

The first night of service, the first lesson was "Why must I be saved, "based on the Scripture, St. John 3:3. More than 70 people visited those blessed classes. Some were saved, others were baptized in the Holy Ghost, others healed and others were delivered from demonic spirits. We all had our experience in spiritual warfare, repentance and sanctification. Our humble beginnings taught us how to honor God in all areas of our lives. We maintained the Bible study for one year and four months, each Tuesday night at 7:00 p.m.

During this time, we called ourselves Neal Street Church because that was the name of the street. We rented space from Mr. and Mrs. Jessie Burns of Clinton, Mississippi, who owned the Agape Community Center. Presiding Elder Jimmie C. and Mrs. Hicks were some of the first persons to commit to sending $20.00 a month to support this move of God.

On Thursday, November 24, 1994, in the 104th Annual Conference, under the leadership of Bishop Joseph Johnson, Sister Bessie Martin, a Traveling Minister, gave her report. As a traveling minister, she started out with a Bible study and now has a total of sixteen members.

Following her report, Bishop Johnson stated that she had gone out and gotten enough members to start a new society. Bishop Johnson entertained a motion that the persons who are attending this mission will become a new society named Neal Street A.M.E. Zion Church, of which Sister Bessie Martin would become the pastor. The motion was made by Presiding Elder Jimmie C. Hicks and seconded by Rev. Willie Cable. Motion carried and was so ordered.

On Mother's Day, May 10, 1995, just as God promised, the bible study turned into our first church service. We were overjoyed by the favor that God had given us with twenty-five people in attendance. The worship service was wonderfully blessed with four souls that came to the Lord. The first eight months in the history of Neal Street A.M.E Zion Church, worship service was held on the second and fourth Sunday of each month. In February of 1996, our church developed fulltime worship.

Our first Quarterly Conference of Neal Street A.M.E. Zion Church was held on Tuesday, March 19, 1996 at 7:00 p.m. in the Agape Community Center, Presiding Elder Jimmie C. Hicks, presiding.

After devotion, Pastor Bessie Martin introduced Elder Hicks as the Presiding Elder of Canton-Jackson District. Elder Hicks called the Quarter to order. Elder Hicks also exhorted the church with words of praise and wisdom for the work that had been done for the Kingdom of God. Presiding Elder Hicks used this quarter as a basic training session, to organize the Quarterly Conference and install officers of the church. It was motioned by Pastor Bessie Martin that the officers be installed as the beginning of Neal Street A.M.E Zion Church.

Near the end of 1996, the owners of Agape Community Center approached Pastor Martin with an opportunity to purchase the building for $75,000 dollars. Bishop Joseph Johnson challenged the membership to raise $10,000.00 and he would match it for the down payment of the building. In 1997, we became the proud owners of the Agape Community Center which officially became Neal Street A.M.E. Zion Church.

In the Annual Conference of 1997, the church name was changed from Neal Street A.M.E. Zion Church to Tabernacle of Grace A.M.E. Zion Church.

Children have always been Pastor Martin's passion, therefore, she and the members started a children's ministry involving the community's children. Resulting from this outreach, an after school program was organized and funded by the State of Mississippi. Pastor Martin served as Director with eight employees.

This program was funded from 1999 to 2001 and served more than eighty children in the surrounding communities. The program consisted of the following: Computer Lab, Meals, Trips, Supplies, Music Teacher, Math Teacher, Transportation, etc. The program also paid for the use of space in the church.

After the funding ended, Tabernacle of Grace organized the GED program funded by Hinds Jr. College. Through the Power of God and teaching and preaching the Word of God, many souls were saved; many healings took place, demons were cast out, and many were filled with the Holy Ghost. The church continued to grow and the favor of God rested upon the place.

The most amazing experience as pastor of Tabernacle of Grace was this: Many of the members were without jobs, some lived on welfare, others delivered from drugs, yet there was no financial lack. We were always able to meet all obligations with very little help from the conference. We were poor in material goods, but rich in faith, and God never failed to come through.

After years of labor, the Spirit of God spoke to my heart that it was time to go. In the 2006 Annual Conference, under the leadership of Bishop Louis Hunter, I stepped down as pastor of Tabernacle of Grace A.M.E. Zion Church. It was after I stepped down that I understood why. Of the twelve years of pastoring, my husband visited the church not more than five times. After stepping down, he surrendered his life to the Lord, attends church every Sunday and is very active in Sunday school.

God said in His Word "My thoughts are not your thoughts, neither are your ways my ways, saith the Lord."(Isaiah 55:8).

God said in His Word "My Thoughts are not your thoughts, neither are your ways My ways, saith the Lord, Isaiah 55:8."

VICTORY AME ZION CHURCH – 1997-2013
PASTOR: Rev. Aurelia Jones-Smith

Having been given a vision to start a new ministry, Rev. Gary D. Adams, Sr. was given a paper appointment by Bishop Nathaniel Jarrett in November 1997, during the 105th session of the South Mississippi Annual Conference at St. Paul AME Zion Church in Canton, Mississippi. The church was organized as Victory A.M.E. Zion Church and the first official church meeting was held at the home of Mr. and Mrs. Estell Green. At that time, eight adults and four children joined the society. Bible Class was held at the Green's home and shortly thereafter, the church was moved to the Southwest YMCA located on Flowers Drive in Jackson, Mississippi.

In October 1999, the church moved to Clinton, Mississippi and began worshipping with Tabernacle of Grace A.M.E. Zion Church where Rev. Bessie Martin served as the pastor. Souls prospered while sharing in the Tabernacle of Grace ministry. Praise teams from both churches sang under the leadership of Mrs. Marietta Johnson.

The church began renovating a building in Jackson, located at 800 Cooper Road in January 2001 and occupied it in March 2001. Every member participated in the renovation project, including the children, who helped with painting. During that period, a television broadcast ministry and a Married Couples ministry were added in addition to computer classes. Moreover, during the Advent and Nativity season, Christmas caroling was done as efforts were made to reach out and connect with the surrounding neighborhood.

In anticipation of purchasing a building located on McFadden Road in Jackson, the lease at 800 Cooper Road was terminated in May 2002; however, due to issues concerning the McFadden Road building's title, in June 2002 an alternative of temporarily leasing space from Covenant Christian Church located at 715 Cooper Road in Jackson was sought. Upon securing a lease with Covenant Christian Church, worship services and Bible Study were begun in the church's fellowship hall. During that period, sheep were continually added to the fold. To heighten a spirit of fellowship, the children's Sunday Church School class was combined with that of Covenant Christian Church's. Additionally, the congregants of both churches regularly fellowshipped by sharing meals.

Shortly following Victory's move to 715 Cooper Road, Covenant Christian Church made a decision to place the church on the market. Recognizing that the Lord had opened a window of opportunity, efforts were begun to pursue purchasing the property. Although membership numbers were small, the faith of the membership was mighty. By fervent and effectual prayer, the assistance of the A.M.E. Zion Church Connection, including, Bishop Jarrett, Presiding Elders and other local churches, necessary funds and financing were obtained to secure the property. Victory began occupying the property on the first Sunday in January 2003.

Over time, other ministries were added and organizational departments of the A.M.E. Zion Church became fully operational. Victory continued serving the Lord and His people with the mission of reaching and offering persons from all walks of life an opportunity to experience the love and saving grace of Jesus Christ, that each might be empowered to live victoriously through the hearing and doing of the word of God. Her motto remains, Achieving Victory Through the Word of God.

Rev. Adams, continued to serve as the pastor of Victory until February 2007, when under the leadership of Bishop Louis Hunter, Sr. Rev. Juanoana D. Portis was appointed to serve as the church's second pastor. Following Rev. Portis' pastoral service, Rev. Roderick Briggs, Sr. was appointed in February 2009 by Bishop Darryl B. Starnes, Sr. Rev. Briggs served as the church's pastor until October 2013, where, during the 123rd session of the South Mississippi Annual Conference, Rev. Dr. Aurelia Jones-Smith was appointed by Bishop Mildred B. Hines to serve as the church's fourth pastor.

Each pastor brought to Victory his or her unique spiritual gifts, pastoring and preaching style, passion, and a love for serving the Lord by ministering to His people. Adding to such, a congregation of God's people walking in the spirit of love, Victory has blossomed into a full-service church that continues to be a beacon shining forth, sharing the gospel, the good news, that is, the hope of salvation through Jesus the Christ.

ZION HILL A.M.E. ZION CHURCH – 1864-2013
PASTOR: Rev. Melvin Blackmon

Zion Hill A.M.E. Zion Church was said to have been started as a campground church, at a place in the Zion Hill area, where slaves used to meet, called "The Camp." Around 1864, after freedom came, the freed slaves and freemen set up the church and called it, the "Camp Ground Church."

The name was changed to "Zion Hill A.M.E. Zion Church" of the Episcopal Methodist Church as written on the deed, and it was moved to the ten acres on which it now sits. On February 10, 1877, the trustees of Zion Hill Church, Green H. Russell, Hal Bryant, and Josiah Gray, entered into an "Indenture" with Peter Battle and his wife, Mary Ann Battle, under the Homestead Law

The trustees bargained with the Battles and the Battles sold this section of property to the church and their successors in office for the use of the land. This was to include the land and all appurtenances on it. At that time the price of land was $4.50 cents an acre. They paid Peter and Mary Battle $50.00 for the ten acres for the church site.

The Church, Zion Hill African Methodist Episcopal Zion Church, remains on the same ten acres to this day.

It was said that the first person to attend a general conference from Zion Hill was Green Russell who attended a conference in New York. Later Henry Russell, the son of Green Russell, was very instrumental in helping the church move forward.

Some of the original founders are buried in the old Zion Hill Cemetery. It was set up for slaves of the Triplett Plantation and their descendants. Several of them still have recognizable headstones. The cemetery is maintained by families of the original founders.

The first meeting place was a bush-harbor. A bush harbor is an open area where bushes, vines, and branches are bent over and connected to form a canopy covering.

Zion Hill in the 50's

This bush-harbor was located at a nearby site on the land from the present church site. It is believed that sometime, between 1877 and 1879 the first church building was built on the same site as the present church, but facing east. There were no outhouses for this church and everyone had to go to the "bushes" to relieve themselves.

The ladies went on one side of the church and the men went on the other. It was not until the late 1940's that the first outhouses were built. The ladies outhouse was later moved to another spot on the same side of the church, and "remodeled" when a cement floor was built for it.

Boys: left-right: Jerry Battle & Harry Crouther

All water for the church was brought from a spring. Mr. Fletcher Whittington was instrumental in getting a pump put in for the church in the mid 40's. He also repeatedly mentioned that the original cemetery was too far from the church and eventually the men of the church agreed and a new area for the cemetery was set aside beside the church.

The first building remained until the late 1930's or early 1940's. The second church was built at this time. The descendants of the original trustees built the second church.

Some of the builders were, Lee Crouther, J. C. Crouther, Arthur Battle, Jim (Doc) Battle, Hillman Douglas, Bill Douglas, Yancy Shell, George Dotson, Nathanial Triplett and their families.

Many times the members of the church did not have money to pay the pastor, especially during the depression. Therefore, he was often paid in foodstuffs, potatoes, syrup, eggs and other items.

Many people walked to church, others came riding mules or horses or in wagons and eventually on the beds of trucks. Cars were a luxury that country people did not have.

In the heat of summer, windows were opened and hand fans were liberally used. In winter there was a wood burning stove in the church to supply some heat. On the fourth Sunday in June, Children's Day, and the fourth Sunday in August, the start of revival, there would be so many people at the church you could barely get on the grounds. Some people would pull their wagons up to the windows to hear the service because they could not get into the church.

There was no electricity so during revival, John Crouther provided a metal lamp with a lantern inside to produce light. Only two people were allowed to handle it, but it was eventually stolen. The church bought another light and it was also stolen. It is not known how many lamps were bought and stolen.

The first original records for Zion Hill, that have been found so far, other than deeds, were made starting in the 1930's with some quarterly conference records. One of the ministers for Zion Hill during the time of the first church was Rev. D. S. Williams. It was stated by one of the members, deceased now, that one fourth Sunday they had service and when the minister returned for service the next fourth Sunday, a new church stood where the old one had been. I believe this was the transition from the first to the second church building.

A list of the officers, of the church in 1947 included: J. L. Crouther, A. D. Battle, Jim Bryant, George Dotson, Yancy Shell, Lee Crouther, J. C. Crouther, Essie Sutton, Christine Battle, Jessie Crouther, Florence Whittington, Annie Lee Harris, Eugene Crouther and G. F. Whittington.

Some of the ministers for Zion Hill during the time of the second church building were: Rev. John Roberts, Rev. B. J. Williams, Rev. C. Goodloe and Rev .Mrs. Mary Coleman. Several of the presiding elders were: Rev. Victory, O. G. Bryant, Rev. Rambert and Rev. D. S. Williams. Two bishops visited Zion Hill during this time: Bishop Taylor visited Zion Hill in the 1940's. Bishop Spottswood visited and delivered a sermon on July 13, 1952. The minister would often visit the home of one of the members on Pastoral Sundays after service and eat dinner with the family. If they had to spend the night, it would be at one of the member's home because there were no other accommodations.

Arthur Battle was the reason Zion Hill started having Sunday school. He was very diligent in coming to church for years on Sunday mornings for Sunday school even when there was little or no participation. Eventually his diligence paid off and Zion Hill started having regular Sunday school on every Sunday morning around 1950. He remained the Sunday School Superintendent until he resigned because of age and illness.

During the time of Rev. Mrs. Mary Coleman, in the 1950's, the first piano was purchased, and the first choir was started with Willie Evans as pianist. Also during her tenure as pastor, the third and last church building was built. Some of the same people who helped build the second church, along with their children, built the third church.

The quarterly conferences were very different at this time. When the Presiding Elder came, it was the same as a regular Sunday service. There were officers and members present. They would have singing, praying, and a sermon was given by the Presiding Elder. After the church service was over, the business session was conducted.

Zion Hill had Sunday school every Sunday, but church service only on the fourth Sunday in the month. This was a general rule then for Black churches in this area. Not only did your church members come to service, but members of other churches and the surrounding community came to visit your church on your service day. Different churches in the area had one service a month. Each church knew the Sunday for every other Church service. This was also true for revivals. Revival at Zion Hill was, and still is, the fourth Sunday in August. There was visiting back and forth between churches on the different service Sundays and during revival.

There were few other social outlets for Blacks during this time of segregation that was acceptable to church members, other than church and school functions. The church was a gathering place, not only for service, but also as a social gathering place for youth and adults alike.

Some of the trustees of Zion Hill were primary supporters of the integration movement.

They met with other integration leaders and registered their church members and other members of the community to vote. One of them, Lee Crouther, was also the first Black School Board Member for Leake County.

Many of the youth were gone and the church membership began to decline. Some of the ministers after Rev. Mary Coleman were: Rev. Craigs, Rev. Charles Beaman, Rev. James Ollie, Rev. Annie Tolbert, Rev. Rebecca Gross, Rev. Small, Rev. Bonnie Travis, Rev. Vaughn Burkes, Rev. Herman Coleman, Rev. Briggs and the present pastor who was also a pastor here in the 1980's, Rev. Melvin Blackmon (picture: page 58 with wife). Several of the Presiding Elders were Rev. E. M. Bryant, Rev. C. W. Speights, Rev. Curtis Brown, Rev. Jimmie C. Hicks, Rev. John C. Evans, Jr., and the present Rev. Gary D. Adams.

Zion Hill, for a long time, was a full thriving church. After integration, more opportunities for Blacks opened up. Many of the children of the church became more educated, and skilled, and moved away for better paying opportunities. The membership declined to as low as eight people with only five attending regular.

The first fellowship hall was an addition to the church in 2002-2003. It included a kitchen, which the church had never had before. On the days when dinner was served at the church, which was always on the fourth Sunday in June, Children's Day, and the fourth Sunday in August, the start of revival, the ladies of the church cooked and brought the food to church with them from home. After service, benches were placed outside the church and dinner was served by the ladies from their "boxes or wash tubs" in front of the church.

By 2004, the first bathroom, with indoor plumbing, built in the late 1960's was replaced. When hurricane Katrina came through in 2005, the winds caused a tree to fall behind the church onto the fellowship hall. Most of it had to be replaced during 2005-2006.

From 2001 to the present, the membership has increased and decreased with deaths of older members and youth coming and going. At present there are twenty two members. Rev. Melvin Blackmon is the present pastor.

I would like to thank the following people for helping me obtain information for this history: *Harold Crouther, Margaret Manntella Gauze,, Mary Hall, Henry Battle and Charles Crouther. Laverne Monroe, Zion Hill Historian: Prepared May 5, 2013*

Girl: Imogene Battle; boys left to right: Larry Battle & Harry Battle

Right center:
believed to have been one of the
the first pastors and his wife.

GALLMAN CHAPEL AME ZION CHURCH-1800-2013
PASTOR: Rev. Derrick Baldwin

Gallman Chapel A.M.E. Zion Church was originated and founded as a "brush harbor" in the year 1800 across Highway 51. The church, having been built by a group of alcoholics, was first called "Who-da-Thought-It" with a membership of 75.

The members then built a wooden structure and named the church Morning Star under the first pastor, Rev. Nash. In 1924, the church was moved to its' present

Location, Old Highway 51, and became Gallman Chapel African M e t h o d i s t Episcopal Zion Church.

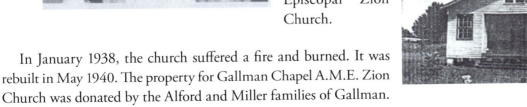

In January 1938, the church suffered a fire and burned. It was rebuilt in May 1940. The property for Gallman Chapel A.M.E. Zion Church was donated by the Alford and Miller families of Gallman.

1952, the Reverend Earnest Athley built the church parsonage. The present structure was renovated, bricked, and the cornerstone was laid in 1974 under Reverend Jimmie C. Hicks. During the summer of 1984 Gallman Chapel A.M.E. Zion Church was renovated under the leadership of Reverend Bennie Luckett.

109 attend summer vacation Bible school

Elder Hicks & Member at Quarterly Conference

Rev. Willie Cable (pastored Gallman Chapel thirty years)
preaches Women's Day Sermon

ST. JAMES AFRICAN METHODIST EPISCOPAL
ZION CHURCH – 1879-2013
Pastor: Rev. Quinton Hicks

St. James A.M.E. Zion Church is located at 53 Wyche, Tallulah, Louisiana, and is pastored by Rev. Quinton Hicks.

The history of Saint James African Methodist Episcopal Zion Church dates back to 1879 under a bush harbor. In 1884, on Montgomery Plantation, Madison Parish, Louisiana, God inspired members continued to worship under a bush harbor. Under the care of Reverend James Inges, an edifice was constructed.

The spiritual overseer was definitely a pioneer during that era because he stepped out on new soil for the purpose of building God's Church.

Many changes were made through the years. The church had its first cornerstone laid in 1899 under the direction of Reverend J. T. Thomas. Several ministers had the privilege of remodeling, tearing down, and moving the church from one location to another for various reasons.

Rebuilt under the Reverend D.D. Nash; rebuilt under the leadership of Reverend C. Tate 1944-1949, which at that time was moved from rural Montrose Plantation, Madison Parish, to Tallulah, Louisiana on Griffin Street in a section of town passionately called the "Fair Grounds."

The present edifice was built under the leadership of the late Reverend W. J. Neal in 1959, and held it's re-opening May 12-17, 1959. The worshippers were exalted in spirit to be in a new place to offer praises to the Lord.

The church has been served by numerous bishops, presiding elders, and pastors. The names of some of the Bishops are Charles U. Tucker, Spottswood, Rueben L. Speaks, Alfred White, Joseph Johnson, Nathaniel Jarrett, Louis Hunter, and Darryl Starnes. Our present Presiding Bishop is the Reverend Mildred B. Hines.

The names of some of the past presiding elders and pastors are Reverend D. S. Williams, B. S. Anderson, D. Nash, Granson, Biry, G. Garner, W. Rice, D. S. Singleton, McGee, F. C. Tate, Triggs, Holmes, Jimmie C. Hicks, Robert Berry, Charles Darden, Fred Brown, Jimmy Harvey, Harvest T. Wilkins, Linda Tobias and Willie E. McKenny. Our present Presiding Elder is Reverend Gary Adams, Sr.

Under the guidance of Reverend Jimmie C. Hicks, the church held its mortgage-burning ceremonies on October 29, 1967. This edifice was also adorned with new furniture, the adjacent lot was purchased, and this structure received an interior and exterior facelift.

The spring of 1997, portions of the building suffered damage by fire due to lightning strikes. The fellowship hall and choir loft were extended and new facilities added under the leadership of Reverend Jimmy Harvey.

We are presently enjoying the spiritual leadership of our loving and devoted Pastor, Reverend Quinton Hicks. Under his guidance, the Saint James African Methodist Episcopal Zion Church continues to grow spiritually in stewardship, knowledge, and worship.

He's the lily of the valley; the bright and morning star; everybody ought to know who Jesus is.

THE CANTON-SHARON DISTRICT

The Canton- Sharon District is lead by Presiding Elder John C. Evans, Jr. Rev. Evans is a native of Hallsboro, North Carolina. He is the son of the late John C. Evans, Sr. and Sarah Elizabeth Evans. He serves as pastor and founder of Cathedral A.M.E. Zion Church, in Jackson, Mississippi.

Dr. Evans is married to Marion Evans. He is the proud father of a son, John C. Evans, III, and daughter, Jessica Dorene Evans.

His educational pursuits include: Elizabeth City State University where he received a Bachelor of Science Degree, Hood Theological Seminary, a Master of Divinity Degree, and Southwestern Christian Theological Seminary, a Doctor of Ministry. He has done additional studies at Wesley Biblical Seminary in Jackson, Mississippi and Memphis Theological Seminary in Memphis, Tennessee. He was awarded an Honorary Doctor of Divinity Degree from Livingstone College.

Dr. Evans presently serves as the Episcopal Prayer Coordinator for the Southwestern Delta Episcopal Area, which includes the States of Arkansas, Louisiana, Oklahoma, South Mississippi, Texas, and West Tennessee-Mississippi. Churches he oversees in the District are:

St. Paul – Canton	Sharon Chapel
Lees Chapel	Greater Sims
Owens Chapel	Sharpsburg
Free Chapel	Jerusalem Temple

ST. PAUL AME. ZION CHURCH – 1847-2013
PASTOR: Rev. Dr. Floyd E. Chambers

"Ye are the light of the world, a city which sits on a hill cannot be hid; let your light so shine before men that they may see your good works and glorify your Father which is in Heaven."

St. Paul A.M.E. Zion Church is Located at 505 South Union Street, Canton, Mississippi, and spearheaded by the "fiery Preacher" Of the South Mississippi Conference, Rev. Dr. Floyd E. Chambers.

The foundation of St. Paul A.M.E. Zion Church was laid in 1847 when a God-sent missionary preacher named Rev. **Granderson Simms (left),** came from Alabama and organized an A.M.E. Zion Church under an old oak tree. Among his membership were a group of slaves: Janette Roach, Ephram Falls, Harriett Sims, Elijah Sims and Mr. Crawfitt, who were brought from the State of Virginia to the City of Canton. They held their meetings under the old oak tree that stood on the lot adjoining Sister Jamimie Jackson's lot, situated on the corner of Hickory Alley and South Street, (South Dinkins Street). This section of the City of Canton was commonly called "Frog Town" and was the slave quarters, described as a "lively area," located in the Miller Subdivision of the Calhoun Addition to the City of Canton.

Priscilla Johnson, also called Mama Cilla, by her children and grandchildren, who was a devout member of St. Paul A.M.E. Zion Church, and a direct descendant of Granderson Simms, gave the above history of St. Paul.

Another version of the history of St. Paul is told by Mrs. Eliza Love. Mrs. Love was also a devout and faithful member of St. Paul A.M.E. Zion Church, and the mother of the late Mr. Edward Love and **Mrs.** Joanna Ratliff. Ms. Ratliff was an ardent Sunday school student and class leader. Sister Love was Secretary of St. Paul A.M.E. Zion Church during the 1930's. Her daughter, Mrs. Joanna Ratliff found a ledger of the church among her keepsakes that provided the following information: "This is the history of St. Paul A.M.E. Zion Church of Canton, Mississippi as I have received it from those who were in the organization. It was on this wise that St. Paul A.M.E. Zion Church was organized by Elder Murphy, a missionary Presiding Elder in the year 1877, under an oak tree between Sister Jamimie Jackson's lot and Dinkins Street, the same year the Canton District was organized under Bishop Jones. Rev. Granderson Simms was the Pastor, Presiding Elder, Rev. Murphy. Rev. Wallace Jones, Rev. Scurlock and Rev. B. J. Adams, were the officiating ministers."

The development of St. Paul depicts it as a log cabin on the location shown as Miller Subdivision in the Calhoun Addition of the City of Canton, Mississippi, recorded on the official city map by George and Dunlap, surveyors in 1898. No documents were found to show how the land for the 1847 log cabin church was obtained. However, this may only reflect the status of record keeping during this period. The absence of land records may also reflect a common practice of the period when Blacks were allowed to build their houses of worship on land they did not or could not own. Also from these records in the Chancery Clerk's office, St. Paul may have moved from its original log cabin structure on Hickory Alley and South Street to its present location on South Union Street.

Who is it that can deny that Granderson Simms did in fact come from Alabama and establish a church in Canton, Mississippi with a group of slaves under an old oak tree in 1847?

Who is it that can deny that a missionary presiding elder named Rev. Murphy organized a church called St. Paul under the same oak tree, on the same lot on or next to Sister Jamimie Jackson on Hickory Alley and South (Dinkins) Street; neither do we have a record of Rev. Granderson Simms works. He is listed among the ministers who were in the organization of the West Tennessee and Mississippi Conference. In1869, Rev. Granderson Simms and William Murphy were in this organization.

The structure was remodeled and made into a two-story building by Rev. J. W. Bennett.

In 1974 St. Paul was completely demolished and a new brick building was built under the pastorate of Rev. J. W. McKinnis.

St. Paul built in 1914. After the log cabin structure

The 1914 building was remodeled into a two story structure in 1942.

Left to right: Bro. Harold Lloyd, Bro. Sammy Glover, Rev. R. M. Richmond, Atty. John H. Nichols, Rev. J. W. McKinnis and Bro. Hatten Sample. (Groundbreaking for 1974 new building)

<u>**Trustees**</u>

John A. Nichols, Chairman; Thomas Johnson, Vice Chairman; H. B. Cooper, Ruby Davis, Secretary; Hatten Sample, Treasurer; R. M Mackey, Annie Devine, James E. Johnson; Rev. S. M. Taylor, Presiding Elder; Mrs. Ethel Coleman, Episcopal Supervisor and the Rt. Rev. C. R Coleman, Bishop.

Stewards
Sammie Glover, Harold Lloyd, Theon Johnson, Alease Lloyd, Clerk, Richard Nichols, Will R. Johnson, and William Johnson

Down through the years, the Lord has been good to St. Paul. He has sent teachers and preachers after His own heart and provided the church with outstanding leadership. Rev. R.M. and Mrs. Ellen Richmond pastured St. Paul during the late 40's and early 50's. St. Paul enjoyed a very large, lively and active youth membership.. Rev. Richmond was dearly loved by all, especially the youth, and he inspired their commitment and participation in the life of the Church. Choirs were youth and senior. The Varick Christian Endeavor Society (VCE) was very active. Mrs. Richmond started a kindergarten that was famous in the community, and many children from other churches attended.

Rev. Samuel Martin (Barbara) Taylor served forty years and is the longest tenured pastor. He was married to Barbara who died and later he married Ruth. By the grace of God, Rev. Taylor kept the church stable when there were only a faithful few members and even fewer resources. He was respected as a good church administrator. He was also known to deliver the shortest sermons, ten minutes at the most. Worship services were brief, yet sacred. Choirs were Senior, Youth, Mass and Buds. Each had their Sunday to lead the worship service.

Rev. Taylor organized Stewardess Board No. 2, which consisted of women not involved in any of the other auxiliaries. God used their gifts to provide unity, financial and spiritual support and to undergird church projects. Assistant ministers were: Rev. G. L. Johnson and Rev. Annie Tolbert.

In the November, 1987 Annual Conference, St. Paul received the first home-grown pastor, Rev. Curtis Brown who was appointed by Bishop Rueben Speaks. His gifts included: preaching, singing, and playing the piano. He operated his own backhoe and ran his own cows.

He came in with a purpose. The church raised $10,000.00 in the first rally. Many souls were saved and baptized and backsliders returned to the fold. The church had a vital Sunday school, Bible study, Varick Christian Endeavor Society, and practiced additional spiritual disciplines such as shut-ins and prayer meetings on a regular basis.

Rev. Brown previously pastored a number of churches in the South Mississippi Conference. He was well known, loved and admired for his humble, quiet spirit, and singing style. He had a high tenor, soulful voice, that would "tear up the church", with songs such as "He's Sweet I Know, By the Grace of the Lord I've Come a Long Way, and He Touched Me."

His wife, Mrs. Hazel Brown also had a quiet, humble spirit, and was very effective organizer. Under her leadership, the Young Adult Usher Board flourished.

Dramatic and extensive improvements were made to the church, some of which are: installation and paving a parking lot, new chandelier lights in the Sanctuary, acquisition of several houses in close proximity to the church was used for rental property and remodeling of the original parsonage into a rental property. Addition of thirty feet was added to the front of the church extending the sanctuary ten feet and adding a spacious vestibule and two large restrooms to accommodate men and women. New carpet and tile was installed in the sanctuary. The tile was donated by Mrs. Eloise Johnson; A heated baptismal pool was installed. A word processor was donated, and a typewriter and Xerox machine were purchased. The kitchen was equipped with a new stove and two buses were purchased by the church. A van was donated to the church by Mr. Joseph Greenhouse to aid in transporting members and/or prospective members to services and other church activities. The roof was replaced on the entire church building. The church property was expanded to include several adjourning lots, and a new ninety-foot long family life center erected.

Five choirs were in place to render sacred music which included Senior, Youth, Inspirational, Male and Buds choirs. The buds choir consists of eighty-five little buds, all blooming for Jesus. Assistant Ministers: Bro. Edward Dunigan, Rev .Clora T. Handy, Sis. Barbara Devine Russell, Sis Peggy Mc Kenny, Sis. Carrie Bennett, and Rev Willie McKinley.

St. Paul Family Life Center

True to our heritage as the Freedom Church, St. Paul has always been actively involved in the community affairs and serve as a favorite meeting place for community organizations. Candidates for public office seek the support and endorsement of St. Paul. The church was instrumental in the election of the first female Mayor, Alice Scott, who is also the first African American Mayor of the City of Canton. Rev. Brown was the official Spiritual Advisor for her campaign.

God has blessed St. Paul over the years with a panorama of "firsts" in various endeavors: H. B. Cooper, first African American Alderman in the City of Canton, Attorney John Nichols, first African American to run for mayor, Larry Fleming, first African American Fireman; Annie Pearl Smoot-Smith, first to own an Adult Day Care Facility in the city of Canton, and Rev. Barbara Devine Russell, first African American Secretary of the Madison County Democratic Party Executive Committee.

God also chose a member of St. Paul to be one of America's foremost civil rights activist, that gained national acclaim as a Mississippi Challenger in the famous 1964 Mississippi Challenge. a move which facilitated the passing of the 1964 Civil Rights Act and the 1965 Voting rights Act.

God chose three Aldermen for the City of Canton out of St. Paul: Preacher's Steward Robbie Johnson Chairman of the Trustee Board, Willie Earl Nichols and Assistant Minister Sammie Brown, who served as Alderman-at-Large.

St. Paul abounded in Christian Service to the community in the following ministries: A Live radio broadcast every first and third Sunday on WMGO Radio Station; Children's Church and Nursery, partner with the Stew Pot by providing space in the family life center to serve over one hundred-fifty needy individuals and families hot, nutritious, lunches five days a week throughout the year; Summer Free Lunch Program which served children ages one to eighteen years old, daily lunches, five days a week, during summer vacation; followed by daily Bible Study; Prison Ministry was conducted, every first and fifth Sunday. Home-made Christmas dinner served to prison participants and gifts of personal items distributed annually; Community Bread Basket: over one hundred families delivered bags of groceries monthly. Senior Citizens Christmas Program. Seniors of the church and community receive Christmas Baskets of fruit and other goodies; Transportation Ministry which transported children and adults to Sunday school, Church services and Bible study, weekly: Two vans ran each Sunday, picking up children and adults for Sunday school and Sunday morning worship services.

Rev. Brown was stricken with leukemia after pastoring St. Paul for seven years. Over fourteen thousand dollars ($14,000) was raised in a special benefit for him. His fiery trial of illness lasted for seven years until he went home to be with Jesus. He served as pastor of St. Paula total of 14 years. His body reposes at his home on Hwy 16 West, in the City of Canton. His love for God, the church, family and community will be cherished and remembered. Rev. Clora T. Handy was the assistant pastor during his illness.

Board of Trustees:
Willie Earl Nichols, Chairman, Perry Cartlidge, Margaret Glove, Ella Johnson, Richard Nichols, Thomas Johnson, Henry Tate, Robbie Johnson, Russell Hamblin, Billie R. Anthony, Secretary

Steward Board:
Robbie Johnson, Preacher Steward, Cleveland Johnson, Cary Johnson, Will Johnson,   Joseph Greenhouse

Presiding Elder, Jimmie C. Hicks, Missionary Supervisor, Mrs. Dorothy Johnson, Rt. Reverend Joseph Johnson, Bishop

Rev. Bennie Luckett was the next pastor sent to St. Paul. It was during the turbulent times of change and grief over the illness and death of Rev. Curtis Brown. He was brought out of retirement after serving for 40 years as pastor of Greater Murphy Chapel A.M.E. Zion Church in Camden, Mississippi.

During his brief tenure of three months, Rev. Luckett preached an uncompromising Gospel message, and steered the church on a steady course through peaceful waters of healing.

Then God sent Rev. Andre' Grant to Pastor St. Paul. He came in with a vision and a purpose. He was a high-powered, fast-paced, super administrator. He moved with lightning speed to reorganize the church and bring it into the Twenty-First CenturyTechnological age. The church exploded financially and numerically. A new remote sound system was installed and a sound room with state-of-the-art recording equipment, including video recording and twin projector screens in the sanctuary, an intercom system so the overflow and those tending the nursery could hear the sermon on Sunday mornings, and new remote ceiling fans in the sanctuary.

Outreach Ministry was extended to: Military, Handicapped, and the Elderly.

Worship services were high as the sanctuary choir reached a new level in rendering sacred music under the directorship of a young musician by the name of Kendarious Thompson. The Choir received recognition as the Outstanding Gospel Choir of the Year by the Canton Gospel Music Awards Association.

Rev. Grant envisioned building an educational wing with a chapel which would be annexed to the main church building. But God had other plans for him. He was suddenly swept home to glory in an automobile accident before his vision could be realized. A Bust was presented to the church by the Canton Business League on his behalf.

Rev. Andre Grant

Board of Trustees:
Willie Earl Nichols, Chairman, Joseph Greenhouse, Thomas Johnson, James Johnson, Cornell Johnson, Billie Ruth Anthony, Henry Tate

Officers: Steward Board
Michael Johnson, Preachers Steward, Joseph Greenhouse, David Thomas, Fred Smith, L. M. Forrest, Larry Johnson, Bill Bunch, James Gilbert, William Johnson

Presiding Elder: Rev. Floyd E. Chambers, Missionary Supervisor: Mrs. Ingrid Hunter, Presiding Prelate: Bishop Louis Hunter. Assistant Ministers: Rev. Dr. Belinda Johnson, Ph.D. Rev. Clora T. Handy and Rev. Barbara Russell

Rev. Gary D. Adams, Sr. received the Divine Appointment from Bishop Darryl B. Starnes. Rev. Adams, being a gifted and joyful Bible teacher and preacher, was free spirited and fun loving. He taught St. Paul that serving God is not and should not be boring. Rev. Adams' messages were recorded each Sunday and CD's were made available for study, teaching and outreach evangelistic ministry.

Under Rev Floyd Chambers, the current pastor of St. Paul an educational wing was completed and annexed to the church and family life center. It consists of five classrooms, named after pillows of the church, a chapel, two restrooms, a beautiful women's lounge, pastor's study with restroom, two large restrooms and a janitor's room. Two spacious hall-ways connect the church, educational wing and family life center and provide access and exit from the front and rear of the church and family life center.

Current Elected official: Andrew Grant, Alderman, City of Canton, Rev. Barbara Devine Russell, Chairman, Municipal Election Commission.

St. Paul is now in its One Hundred Sixty-Seven years of existence. Since its beginning in 1847, it has weathered every storm. Many times the faithful few have carried the load.

True to its connection as an African Methodist Episcopal Zion Church, St. Paul stands second to none in loyalty and love for God and Zion. In the course of One Hundred Sixty-Seven Years, the church has moved from a place under an old oak tree to a log cabin built on the same lot to the current edifice on South Union Street.

St. Paul continues to be a light, and a beacon of hope in the Canton and Madison County community, and by the grace of God, with the love of Jesus, and the power of the Holy Spirit, will continue to lift up the mighty Name of Jesus, as we endeavor to exemplify God's worth through praise, worship, fellowship, discipleship and Christian service.

Current: Trustees:

Rev. Floyd E. Chambers, Sis. Billie Ruth Anthony, Johnny Brown, Timothy Chambers, Linda Carroll, Kashaka Fleming, Joseph Greenhouse, Robert Tucker, Joe Wells

Sreward Board:

Napoleon Brooks, Preacher Steward, Barbara Luckett, Toby Lacy, William Johnson, Larry Johnson, Cary Johnson, Shara Johnson, Rev. Andre Grant

Former Pastors 1847 to 1863-

Rev. Granderson Simms, Founder and First Pastor, Rev. N. J. Adams, Second Pastor

Pastors from the 1920's to 1930's:

Rev. E. G. Williams, Rev. Gillespie, Rev. Frazier, Rev. Bennett, Rev. Service, Rev. Williams, Rev. Jones,

Pastors from the 1940's to 1950's:

The Rev. Stitt, Rev. Rev. J. H. McMullin, Rev. Ben Williams, Rev. D. S. Williams, Rev. Alex Sherrod, Rev. H. R. Banks, Rev. Bennett.

Pastors from the early 50's to present:

Rev. W. J. McKinnis, Rev. Raymond M. Richmond, Rev. S.M. Taylor, Rev. Curtis Brown, Rev. Andre' Grant, Rev. Bennie Luckett, Rev. Gary D. Adams, Sr., Rev. Dr. Floyd E. Chambers, current pastor

Presiding Elders

Rev. Jimmie C. Hicks, Rev. S. M. Taylor, Rev. Dr. Floyd Chambers Rev. Jimmie C. Hicks, Rev. John C. Evans, Jr.

Bishops:

Jones, Coleman, Charles Eubank Tucker, Stephen Gill Spottswood, Reuben L. Speaks, Alfred E. White, Joseph Johnson, Nathaniel Jarrett, Louis Hunter, Darryl B. Starnes and our Current Bishop Mildred B. Hines

H. B. Cooper with shovel; Rev. Benjamin Small, Right.

Left-right: Rev. R. M Richmond, Attorney John Nichols,
Thomas Johnson, and Hatten Sample

Left: from left to right: John Nichols, Blanche Nichols,
Annie Devine & Betty Nichols, standing

Upper left: Mrs. Hazel & Rev. Curtis Brown & Mrs. Blanche Nichols. Upper right: Mrs. .Rosie Sutherland and family; mid left: Mrs. Sadie Lee Johnson and Buds; mid right: Mrs. Ruby Davis & family; bottom: Mrs. Blanche Nichols introduces speaker Mrs. R. N. Porter (front seated) at Stewardess Board program On Nichol's right (seated) Linda Faye Rimmer,

left: the Whitehead
Sisters, right: Attorney John Nichols &
son Adam

Mid left: Mrs. Nichols Primary Sunday
school Class. Mid right, Mrs. Blanche
Nichols

Bottom: left: St. Paul beginners class
Bottom right: Nichols children
In Christmas Play

The Nichols Children: (Lt to Rt): Andrea, Alexis
Adam, April & Linda. Center: Left: Benjamin, right;
Richard. Front row: left Ladonna; right Monica

Blanche Nichols rehearses Christmas play with children

Beginners Sunday School Class

Right: Mrs. Blanche Nichols (center)
& two Daughters-in-law: left to right:
Annie Pearl and Betty Nichols

Sister Thea Bowman-Canton's first African
American Catholic Nun Speaks at St. Paul

Rt. Mrs. Blanche Nichols, center,
and daughters-in-law: Annie Pearl
on left and Betty on the right

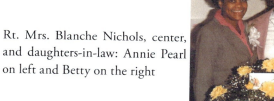

Rev. & Mrs. Curtis Brown & Mrs. Blanche Nichols

Mrs. Minnie Cameron, Mrs. Annie Devine & Mrs. Ethel Turner

Tonjula Chambers & Ladonna Nichols

Catherine Ann Bennett & Son

Left: Thomas (Oop) Johnson

Right: Lynette Nichols

Christina Nichols & Corey Johnson portray Mary & Joseph in Christmas Play

Left: below Johnnie Rogers pins wings on angel

Andrico, Jeremy and Allen, Blackman, Jr. portray shepherds in Christmas Play

Right:
from left:
Three Kings:
Gabriel
Cartlidge
Jeffery Nichols &
Geoffrey
Johnson

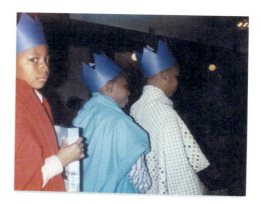

left: front: angel Jalesa Davis, right center:
Whitney Johnson

Christmas play angels. Geoffrey Johnson
Right, second row; Naudia front, left

Annie Pearl Smith (left) & Barbara Devine Russell (right) in front of bell tower, one snowy Sunday Morning

Left: Rev. Curtis Brown & Trustee Perry Cartlidge

St. Paul observes African American History Month

Left: Delores. Anderson, Lynett Nichols, Barbara Devine Russell, Tameka Chambers, Hattie Chambers, Betty Nichols, Andrea Grant & Rachel Johnson

Erica Johnson

Below: left-right: Mildred Watts, Patricia Bennett & Barbara Devine-Russell

Annie Devine recognized for Civil Rights contributions

Left-right: Mrs. Bessie Bunche Catherine Harris & a little brother

Hazel Taylor, and family

left-right: Francesser & Pattria Carter, Gobbrielle Lewis, Shakesha & Rachel Lewis, Oxavia, Frederick & Nicholas Carter; front row: Alicia, Malicia, Isaiah, Teresa & Tyrick Carter (Outreach Children's Ministry) Rev. Barbara Devine Russell's (Easter Sunday morning) Outreach Children's Ministry (Stella Griffin, left)

Asst. Ministers Edward
Dunigan, Clora Handy & Barbara D. Russell

Mrs. Annie Devine

Ms. Barbara Devine Russell

Rev. Barbara Devine Russell leads Sunday Morning worship. Seated: asst. minister Sammy Brown. Pastor (not shown) Rev. Gary D. Adams, Sr.

Alasia Frazier get baptized by Rev. Floyd Chambers. Her mother, Yolanda Francis right rear & Mr. Napoleon Brooks, Preacher's Steward, left rear.

Below: the Sanctuary choir renders high praise in Sunday morning worship

District Missionary Supervisor Monica Johnson Gilkey

Deaconesses Carol Caroll, Linda Caroll & Rosie Brooks (left front. Row)

Glad to be in the service one more time!

Middle row: Mr. & Mrs. Russell Carroll

David Washington

Linda Williams

Bottom-right: Asst. minister: Lynnette Nichols reads Scripture lesson

Left-right: Naudia and Jeremy Walker, Hattie Watts, Bertha Cain (Wimp), Mid row: Children & Youth Choir: bottom row: Mother's day queens left-right: Barbara Carroll, Ola Francis, Martha Scott, and Tommie Fleming Right: Jarvis Brown, front, center as St. Paul worships in giving.

THE STORY OF SHARON CHAPEL AME ZION CHURCH
1874-2013
PASTOR: Rev. Derrick Blue

"And the rain fell, and the floods came, and the winds blew, and beat against that house, yet it did not fall, because it had been founded on the Rock. Matthew 7:25

Rev. Derrick, Sis. Paula and baby Boy Blue

The mid 1870's marked the beginning of Sharon Chapel A.M.E. Zion Church. The church started with a group of Blacks who believed in God and they wanted a place to worship. Rev. Mose Cortney, with neighbors and friends, went from house to house to hold worship services. When the weather was pleasant, these Black Christians would hold services under the shade trees.

Rev. Mose Cortney and citizens of the Sharon community were very instrumental in the establishment of the first Sharon Church. Sharon Chapel Methodist Church was organized in 1874. The church had about thirty members, and Deacon Grander Sims was the first pastor of the church.

Early in the history of Sharon Church, Rev. Mose Cortney, his son, Matthew Cortney, neighbors, and friends raised enough funds to build the first Sharon Church. The first Sharon Church was built with logs and floors on land donated by Rev. Mose Cortney.

Some years later, around 1924, this Church was destroyed by a storm.

In 1924, Rev. John Hilliard was appointed to pastor the Sharon Chapel A.M.E. Zion Church by the A.M.E. Zion South Mississippi Conference. Over one hundred years ago, Sharon Church members learned about the A.M.E. Zion Church. Sharon was basically a family church. Some members wanted to become Zionites and some members did not want to join the South Mississippi Conference. So, the church split up and some members joined the A.M.E. Zion Conference, others joined Old Oak United Methodist Church.

Under the pastoral leadership of Rev. John Hilliard, a second Sharon Chapel A.M.E. Zion Church was built in 1924. This Church was a brick Church built with a pastor's chambers and a pool in the back.

In 1925 Sharon Chapel A.M.E. Zion Church hosted the Annual South Mississippi Conference.

In 1942, the church got behind in its mortgage payment and a "For Sale" sign was placed on the church doors. Then, Madison County took over the property and used the church for a school. Later, this church and school were destroyed by fire. So, in 1958 the school called "Freedom School" was closed. At this time, Rev. Mose Cortney's nearest relative was found. Mary Jane Cortney, and she was given the property and deeds as Rev. Mose Cortney had ordered.

Rev. Clarence Goodloe was appointed pastor of Sharon A.M.E. Zion Church in the early 1940's. Property to build a third Sharon A.M.E. Zion Church was purchased by Tommy and Elsie Reed in 1944. This property was also on Sharon Road, slightly north of the Old Sharon A.M.E. Zion Church. A third Sharon A.M.E. Zion Church was constructed in 1948 under the leadership of Rev. Clarence Goodloe. Rev. Goodloe was the appointed pastor of Sharon Chapel A.M.E. Zion Church for fifteen years. The trustees during that time were: Mr. Eugene Garner, Mr. Percy Lane, Mr. Nathan Mayberry, Mr. Will Greenwood, Mr. Joe Watkins, Sr., Mr. Archie Thurman and Mr. Albert Carson, Sr.

Rev. Benjamin Small was appointed pastor of Sharon A.M.E. Zion Church at the 1966 South Mississippi Conference.

In 1967, the church was remodeled under the leadership of Rev. Small to include inside bathroom facilities.

Sharon Chapel A.M.E. Zion Church
Re-Modeled in 1967

Rev. Small was appointed pastor for seventeen years. Rev. Small raised the first $10,000 to build the current fourth Sharon A.M.E. Zion Church.

In 1985, the Rev. Andrew Griffin was appointed pastor of Sharon Chapel A.M.E. Zion Church.

In 1986, Rev. Jimmie C. Hicks, Presiding Elder, was appointed to pastor Sharon Chapel A.M.E. Zion Church.

December 4, 1986, Rev. Hicks held his first business meeting. He informed members that with the help of God Almighty, we would build a new church. On April 15, 1987, Rev. Hicks called a members meeting to inform the members that the lot the church was currently standing on was one-sided and small. He suggested relocating to build the fourth Sharon Chapel A.M.E. Zion Church.

On February 28, 1988, the members of Sharon Chapel A.M.E. Zion Church purchased property to build a fourth Sharon Chapel A.M.E. Zion Church. The property was slightly north of the location of the third church on Sharon Road. Section 36, Township 10 North Range 3 East. Reservations and restrictions were herein contained to the trustees at that time: Mozell Allen, Jr., Emmitt Sanders, Joe Watkins, Jr., Thomas Douglas, Sylvester Draine, Larry Reed, Floyd Bilbrew, Taylor Lott, Viola Allen, Maggie Sims and Rev. Jimmie C. Hicks.

On March 6, 1988, a Ground **B**reaking Ceremony was held for the construction of the fourth Sharon Chapel A.M.E. Zion Church under the leadership of Rev. Jimmie C. Hicks. Bishop Ruben Lee Speaks spearheaded this Ground Breaking Ceremony.

Under the leadership of Rev. Hicks, a fourth Sharon Chapel A.M.E. Zion Church was built. This church is a brick church with a large sanctuary, a fellowship hall, an in-door pool, a nursery, a choir room, a pastor's study and various other convenient meeting rooms.

On February 19, 1989, an innovative church dedication service was spear headed by Bishop Alfred White, Presiding Elder/Pastor Rev. Jimmie C. Hicks, the members and other A.M.E. Zion Church ministers.

Thanks be to God who continues to bless our church. We extend gratitude to God and to our Great Forerunners. Some of the pastors who have pastored at Sharon A.M.E. Zion Church are:

Rev. Gains	Rev. Byrd
Rev. Oak	Rev. Grocery
Rev. Church	Rev. Hilliard
Rev. Charles Eubanks	Rev. Erlum
Rev. Robinson	Rev. James Ollie
Rev. Horn	Rev. Haynes
Rev. Rice	Rev. D.S. Williams
Rev. Hawthorne	Rev. Clarence Goodloe
Rev. Banks	Rev. Deacon Grander Sims
Rev. Benjamin Small	Rev. Andrew Griffin
Rev. Tucker	Rev. Jimmie C. Hicks

Some of the church's milestones and accomplishments under the leadership of Rev. Dr. Jimmie C. Hicks are:

June 26, 1988 -First Annual Men's Day Program asking men for $200 and women $25.

September 25, 1988 - First Women's Day Program asking women for $200 and men $25.

December 11, 1988 - Sharon Chapel A.M.E. Zion Church became a Station Church, meeting full-time every Sunday of the month, instead of twice a month.

September 18, 1991- Purchased first pearl drums for choir/music department

September 5, 1993 -Church installed its first alarm system.

October 10, 1993 -Installation of the church cornerstone.

January 2, 1994 -Purchased church steeple.

On September 29, 1996 - Jimmie C. Hicks spearheaded the ground breaking for the multipurpose building that included a large fellowship hall and six classrooms

On November 3, 1996 -Church purchased overhead shed for parking.

On April 6, 1997- The Church purchased 32 new A.M.E. Zion Hymnals.

On May 4, 1997- The first Sunday school was held in the multipurpose building.

On June 22, 1997 - The multipurpose building was named The Jimmie C. Hicks Multipurpose Building

In 1998 - The church Motto was adopted: "We are Recruiters for Christ".

April 1999 - Purchased first church van.

In the year 2000 -An Annual Memorial Service was initiated.

In 2001 -The A.M.E. Zion Emblem was matted and displayed in the sanctuary.

On August 11, 2003 -The church monument was dedicated.

On 2004 -The call for all members was: "Love Ye One Another. which hangs all of the Law."

In 2006 -The Rose of Sharon Gymnasium was constructed.

October 22, 2006 - Sharon Chapel A.M.E. Zion Church hosted the 116th South Mississippi Annual Conference under the leadership of Bishop Louis Hunter. The conference was a great success. On Sunday morning, there was a major water leak in Sharon and Sunday morning services were moved to Lee's Chapel A.M.E. Zion Church.

In 2010 - Sharon Chapel A.M.E. Zion Church engaged in a partnership with the Madison County Citizens Services Agency to support the distribution of 100 commodities boxes each month to senior citizens in Madison County. The church donates the space to distribute these boxes as a service to the community. Glory goes to God.

We are grateful today for the founders of our church, the officers, the dedicated members, and most of all the pastors and leaders of this church over the years.

Groundbreaking for 4th Sharon Church lead by Bishop Rueben Speaks (center with Shovel)

Church dedication spearheaded by Bishop Alfred White (center) Rev. Floyd
Chambers center; Pastor Rev. Jimmie C. Hicks front right.

Construction of Parking Garage

Church dedication ceremony lead by Bishop Alfred White
Rev. Floyd Chambers, left, Pastor Rev. Jimmie C. Hicks, right

The Lord's Prayer

Matthew 6:9-13

AFTER THIS MANNER, THEREFORE, PRAY YE
OUR FATHER WHICH ART IN HEAVEN, HALLOWED BE THY NAME.
THY KINGDOM COME. THY WILL BE DONE
IN EARTH, AS IT IS IN HEAVEN.
GIVE US THIS DAY OUR DAILY BREAD;
AND FORGIVE US OUR DEBTS, AS WE FORGIVE OUR DEBTORS.
AND LEAD US NOT INTO TEMPTATION,
BUT DELIVER US FROM EVIL;
FOR THINE IS THE KINGDOM, AND THE POWER, AND THE GLORY,
FOREVER. AMEN

THE HISTORY OF LEES CHAPEL AME ZION CHURCH
EARLY 1900'S - 2013
Pastor: Rev. Henry Brown

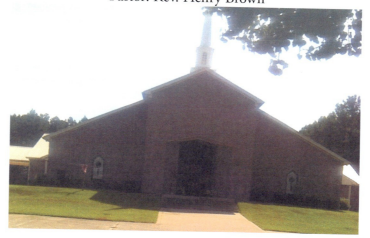

Lees Chapel Groundbreaking Ceremony: (Ft.row: Lt-rt: Presiding Elder Jimmie C. Hicks, Rev. Henry Brown, Pastor and Rev. Dr. Floyd Chambers

In the early 1900's, a man by the name of Frank Sims grew weary of watching his people wasting their lives away gambling in the ditches around the area where this present church stands. He felt if Blacks were ever to improve on the quality of their lives, they must be educated. It was because of this need that Frank Sims conceived the idea of starting a school for Blacks in the area.

Frank Sims, his brother, John Sims, and his nephew, Johnny Sims, arranged to acquire a building for the purpose of being used as a school. They obtained an old house from George Brown which was then moved to the site on which the present Lees' Chapel A.M.E. Zion Church now stands. The building was seated facing the west. This building was used as a school for any children living in the area wishing to get an education. The first teachers for the school were from Leake County. Because the teachers lived so far from the school, they lived in the home of Frank and Ida Sims during the week while they taught classes. Sometimes after the school was started, it was decided to also use the building as a church.

The church was called Sims Chapel, named after the man who provided the building for the church. The first preacher to preach at the newly formed Church was Reverend Ed Williams, who preached on the text, "Who Touched Me?" At this time, there was no one pastor assigned to the church. Various preachers, as they were available, would preach for the congregation.

In November of 1922, Frank and Ida Mae Sims officially deeded the land on which the church was seated to the trustees of the A.M.E. Zion Church. This deed was made with the agreement that the A.M.E. Zion Church would build and maintain upon said land a church and school building and that such building was to be continually used for church and school purposes. At some point, because there was another church in the area also using the name of Sims Chapel, the name of the church was changed to Lee's Chapel after Ed Lee Sims, the son of the church donors, Frank and Etha Sims.

The first pastor to be assigned to Lee's Chapel A.M.E. Zion Church by the AME Zion conference was Reverend Wade Hampton. Between the time when Rev. Hampton was assigned as pastor in 1922 or 1923 to about 1960, several other pastors were assigned to Lee's Chapel Church. These included, but were not necessarily limited to or rendered service in the order listed. Rev. Clarence Goodloe was pastor on two separate occasions. The following is a list of others who have served as pastor of the Lee's Chapel A.M.E. Zion Church:

Rev. W. T. Hawthorne	1960-1979
Rev. Andrew Griffin	1975-1985
Rev. Benjamin Small	1985-1986
Rev. J. P. Phillips	1986-1997
Rev. Charles Darden	June 1997-Nov. 1997
Rev. Henry Brown	1997-Present

The Presiding Elder District names have changed several times. The following have served as Presiding Elders of Lee's Chapel A.M.E. Zion Church: Rev. D. S. Williams, Rev. S. M. Taylor, Rev. Jimmie C. Hicks, Rev. Bennie Luckett, Rev. Floyd Chambers, Rev. Jimmie C. Hicks, Rev. John C. Evans, Jr., Rev. Jimmie C. Hicks, and Rev. John C. Evans, Jr.

Board of Trustees: Walter Lott, B. Collins, Anderson Roberts, Willie Griffin, Charlie Brown, General Sims, Bertha Wilson, J. T. Smith, Walter Luckett, W. K. Luckett, George Sutton, Gloria Luckett, James Parker, Arthur Matlock, Georgetta Black, Leon Fleming, Percy L. Brown, Norris Walker, Eddie Brown, Lee Clayton, and Rev. Henry Brown.

Steward Board: Walter Lott, B. Collins, Anderson Roberts, Willie Griffin, Charlie Brown, General Sims, Bertha Wilson, J. T. Smith, Walter Luckett, W. K. Luckett, George Sutton, Gloria Luckett, James Parker, Arthur Eddie Brown, Lee Clayton, and Rev. Henry Brown.

Sunday School Superintendents: Walter Lott, Percy L. Brown, George Sutton, Bertha Wilson, Lydell Smith, Velma Brown, and Gloria Luckettt.

Sunday School Teachers: Mary Williams, Mary Jones, Doretha Williams, Ruth Scott, Lillle Pickett, George Sutton, Earlene Luckett, Johnny Matlock, Gloria Luckett, Lydell Smith, Quanta Walker, Denisha Edwards, Patricia Parker, Jenetta Hayes, Bretta Blackman, Cleophus Walker, W. K. Luckett, Jr., Steve Johnson, Velma Brown, Rev. Julia Lindsey and Angela Brown.

Deaconess: Mary Luckett, Louise Sims, Lugene Watkins, Geniva Griffin, Lillle Brown, Betsy Roberts, Virginia Sims, Henrietta Williams, Mattie Washington, Lillie Miggins, Betsy Lott, Lucindy Walker, Gloria Luckett, Selete Wilson, and Elizabeth Cleaver.

Lee's Chapel underwent reconstructions in 1979 under the leadership of Rev. Andrew Griffin and again in 2005 under the leadership of Rev. Henry L. Brown.

Lee's Chapel A.M.E. Zion Church has grown substantially through the years. We have about one hundred-seventy members, expanding from three Sunday School classes to now five, (beginners, juniors, intermediate, adult men, adult women.) five choirs, (buds, youth, male, sanctuary, ministers and spouses.) seven class leaders, and a praise dance ministry. We are thankful to Mr. & Mrs. Frank and Ida Sims, for their vision years ago, it has yielded great and positive growth in our church today.

GREATER SIMS AME ZION CHURCH– 1800'S-2013
Pastor: Rev. Dr. Peggy Mckenny
George Washington Drive, Canton, Mississippi

In the 1800's, there was no church located in the Sims community. Presently, this community is located northeast of Canton in rural Madison County on Goodloe Road. Bass Sims, an ex-slave and a citizen of the community gave an acre of land for the purpose of building a church. Once the church was built and organized, it was named Sims Chapel in honor of Rev. Bass Sims.

Rev. Bass Sims married a young lady whose name was Nancy. To this union four children were born; William Sims, Lynch Sims, James Sims, and Bettie Sims Douglas. Lynch Sims followed in his father's footsteps and later became a minister.

It is regrettable that no written church records were kept during that time. However, with the assistance of Mrs. Joanna Ratliff, Mrs. Susie Mackie, Ms. Lula Garrett, Mrs. Lee Ethel Cheeks, and Mr. Willie C. Thomas, Sr., detailed facts relevant to the church history were provided.

In the 1930's, the trustees of Sims Chapel were Mr. William Sims, Rev. Lynch Sims, Mr. Charlie Garrett, Mr. Willie Coleman, Mr. Aaron Thomas, Sr., Mr. Granavel VanBuren, and Mr. Andrew Robinson.

In 1945, the church was destroyed by a wildfire. Members of the community witnessed the fire approaching the church and attempted to extinguish the flames, but unfortunately their efforts were futile. Rev. Charles H. Beamon was the pastor at that time. The congregation worshipped in the home of Rev. Lynch Sims until the church was rebuilt on an acre of land he later donated to church. The new church was built on the same road, but in a different location. That building is still standing on Goodloe Road and is now a part of Jerusalem Temple African Methodist Episcopal Zion Church.

In 1967, the church was renovated under the leadership of Rev. Curtis Brown and was renamed Greater Sims African Methodist Episcopal Zion Church. During this time, the trustees were Mr. Bowman Carter, Mr. Gennie Gibson, Ms. Lula Garrett, Mr. Albert Thomas, Sr., Mr. Percy Stokes, Mr. Leon Grant, and Mr. Willie C. Thomas, Sr. Later, While the church was in that same location, Mrs. Irene Thomas, Mr. Percy Grant, and Mr. Louis Whitehead became members of the Board of Trustees.

In 1985, Rev. Curtis Brown erected a new sanctuary in Canton on the corner of Lutz Avenue and Rick's Drive. During that time, the trustees were Mr. James Stokes chairman, Mr. Willie C. Thomas, Sr. secretary, Mrs. Irene Thomas chaplain, Mr. Percy Grant, Mr. Louis Whitehead, Mr. Henry Chinn, Mr. James C. Smith, Mr. Percy Stokes, Mr. Roosevelt Jackson, and Mr. Genie Gibson. The church secretary was Mrs. Grace Luckett. The new sanctuary was dedicated five years later on January 13, 1990 under the leadership of Rev. Benjamin Small.

In 2006, the present sanctuary was built and completed adjacent to the old building. Rev. Charles Brown was the pastor at that time, and the trustees: Mr. Percy Brooks, chairman, Mr. Willie C. Thomas, Sr. secretary, Mrs. Irene Thomas: chaplain, Mr. James Stokes, treasurer, Mr. Cleo Brooks, Mrs. Rosie Brooks, and Mrs. Brenda Stuckey. The current church secretary, Benae Jackson, was also serving as church secretary at that time.

As far back as memory permits, the ministers who have pastored Sims Chapel have been the following: Rev. Bass Sims, pastor and founder, Rev. T. B. Anderson, Rev. T. S. Sanders, Rev. A. R. Rimmer, Rev. L. K. Owens, Rev. Charles H. Beamon, Rev. John Roberts, Rev. W. T. Tolbert, Rev. John Anderson, Rev. W. T. Hawthorne,

Rev. Clarence C. Goodloe, Rev. John Sims, Rev. James Ollie, Rev. Curtis Brown, Rev. S. M. Taylor, Rev. Andrew Griffin, Rev. Benjamin Small, Rev. Edgar Reed, Rev. Dr. Floyd Chambers, and Rev. Charles Brown. Rev. Gwendolyn Hampton and Rev. Clora T. Handy.

Currently Greater Sims African Methodist Episcopal Zion Church is under the leadership of Rev. Dr. Peggy McKenny.

THIS STORY WRITTEN AND SUBMITTED BY:

MR. WILLIE C. THOMAS, SR.

THIS THIRTY-FIRST (31ST) DAY OF MAY IN THE YER OF OURLORD
TWO THOUSAND AND THIRTEEN (2013)

OWENS CHAPEL AME ZION CHURCH –LATE 1800'S-2013

North Natchez Street

Kosciusko, MS

Rev. Terry White

Owens Chapel A.M.E. Zion Church of Kosciusko, Mississippi has a long and interesting history. It is a history that we hope will remain a part of Kosciusko.

This church began as the Sam Young A.M.E. Zion Church in the late 1800's. It was located on Goodman Street in Kosciusko. The church was donated to us by Rev. W. Owens. In 1932 it was moved to Natchez Street and the name was changed to Owens Chapel. In 1973 it was remodeled by the late Rev. Mary Coleman.

At one time Owens Chapel was the leading Black church in the city of Kosciusko. We have even hosted annual conferences. We are proud of our church and what it means to our community. We have been blessed to have many great pastors and presiding elders to come our way. Thank God for Owens Chapel A.M.E. Zion Church. Some of the former pastors are:

Rev. Paits

Rev. Benjamin Small

Rev. Kelly

Rev. James Olive

Rev. Stitch

Rev. Fred Brown

Rev. Carpenter

Rev. Robert Chambliss

Rev. Holmes

Rev. Gwendolyn Hampton

Rev. Farmer

Rev. Lelar Brooks

Rev. Mary Coleman

Rev. Fred Brown

Rev. J. P. Phillips

Rev. Terry White

Presiding Elders

Rev. Roberts

Rev. Bennie Luckett

Rev. Sam Boyd

Rev. Floyd Chambers

Rev. Speight

Rev. Gary Adams

Rev. Wilkinson

Rev. John Evans

SHARPSBURG AME ZION CHURCH-EARLY 1900'S-2013
Pastor: Rev. Fred Brown

Sharpsburg A. M. E. Zion Church was established in the early 1900's on land donated by the Sharp Family. The church was originally known as "Burksville," but the name was later changed to"Sharpsburg," to honor the Sharp family for their land donation. Church records show that one of the early members, Mrs. Jennie R. Johnson, joined Sharpsburg A.M.E. Zion Church in 1918. The church was rebuilt in 1948, under the leadership of trustees Clay Sharkey, Isadore Glover, John H. Phillips, and Sylvester Glover. Sharpsburg was remodeled in the 1980's during the leadership of John H. Phillips, Trustees Chairman, Rev. Benjamin Small, Pastor.

In 1991, the pastor and the members of Sharpsburg A.M.E. Zion Church decided to build a new church sanctuary. A building fund was established to accomplish this goal and fundraising began during the leadership of Rev. G. L. Johnson. Between 1992 and 1994, under the pastoral leadership of Rev. James Jones, plans for the new church structure began. As funds increased, the Board of Trustees decided construction could begin and the members applied for a loan through Merchants and Farmers Bank in Canton, Mississippi to cover the remaining cost of construction. Trustees signing the loan were: Tracy Steele, Clara Steele, Lillie Lowe, Fleta Esco, Evelyn Warren, and Johnnie S. Brown.

In the summer of 1995, Mr. & Mrs. Mark Shapley donated two acres of land adjacent to the old church for the new church building. With the loan and land secured, construction began later that summer, with George Johnson as the builder. The hard work, dedicated time, and God's grace and mercy guided the minds and hearts of a few faithful servants to gather up what was needed to move forward to completion. The first worship services were held in the fellowship hall in December 1995, as finishing touches were added in the sanctuary. Regular worship service began in the church sanctuary January 7, 1996.

Church leadership was: Presiding Bishop Joseph Johnson, Presiding Elder, Rev. Jimmie C. Hicks, Rev. Fred Brown, Pastor, and Tracy Steele, Chairman of Trustee Board. Members of the trustee board were: Johnnie Brown, Fleta Esco, Annie Elmore, U. S. Johnson, Jr., Lillie Lowe, Leontyne Sims, Clara Steele, and Evelyn Warren.

A cornerstone-laying ceremony, officiated by Anderson Lodge No. 9, of Canton, Mississippi was held July 14, 1996, during the pastoral leadership of Rev. Fred L. Brown. The members of Sharpsburg A.M.E. Zion Church marched from the old church to the new sanctuary. It stands as a testament to the faith of all the dedicated trustees and church members. The previous church building was eventually torn down and hauled off.

FREE CHAPEL AME ZION CHURCH – 1800's-2013
Pastor: Rev. Yolanda Lowe

Free Chapel was established sometime in the eighteenth century, when a plantation owner by the name of Bolder Lott bought slaves from Alabama and brought them back to Mississippi.

Among those slaves was a fifteen-year-old Black girl name Waddie. Waddie married John Collins and they had children whose names were: Dicy, Silas, Jessie, Paul, Mary and Simon. Under the leadership of Bolder Lott, he built a church for his slaves. He named that church "Lottville." He also gave his slaves two acres of land where the church was built. Waddie, John, and some of their children and grandchildren are buried in that cemetery.

After many years of worship services at Lottville, another generation of Waddie's children and grandchildren decided to break the chain that bound them; as a group of dependent people, they wanted to be free.

They formulated a plan to move, so they acquired two acres of land from a Black family, John and Sally Day. They hired a carpenter whose name was Monrow Beamon. He built the church with the assistance of the members. After the church was finished they moved into the church. They knew it was the grace and mercy of God that freed them, so the church had a meeting rejoicing and praising God that broke that slavery chain that bound them and set them free. That's how the church got its name Free Chapel.

Free Chapel has one Annual Day that is celebrated each year, the third Sunday in October. This Day was organized by one of Free Chapel's members, Rev. Silas Byrd, in 1948. This Day is known as Free Chapel's Homecoming. Rev. Silas presided over this program until his health began to fail him, then he passed the responsibility on to his nephew Rev. Thomas Johnson. He presided over this program until his health failed, then he passed the responsibility on to his nephew Rev. Robert Branson, who has faithfully served as Homecoming Pastor since October 1977.

Free Chapel purchased two acres of land from George Green adjacent to the church in 2007.

Free Chapel has had its share of trials and tribulations. In 1958, Free Chapel was damaged by a tornado. The church was restored.

The church bell was taken and never returned. In 1999 some improvements were made to the church. The church was torn down in 2010 and the church lumber and other church property hasn't been accounted for.

Waddie, the fifteen year old slave girl from Alabama is classified as the mother of Free Chapel today. The majority of Free Chapel's members are Waddie's grandchildren. Waddie's generation of ministers from Free Chapel extends through the seventh generation: Her son Silas Byrd and his children: Thomas Johnson, Evan Johnson, Silas Byrd, Jr., Robert Branson, Sr., Robert Branson, Jr., Marion Johnson, Tomaz Adams, Canary Bell, Jackie Thompson, and Amos Branson.

JERUSALEM TEMPLE A.M.E. ZION CHURCH - 2002-2013
PASTOR: REV. SAMMIE BROWN

Let it be known that in February, 2002, Jerusalem Temple was birthed from a driven passion and much prayers through the Holy Spirit, and was formed by God's servant, Sister Peggy V. Mc Kenny, not ordained at the time. June 13, 2002, the first deposit on a building lease was paid at 5420 J. R. Lynch Street Extension, Jackson, Mississippi, leased from Mr. Ed. Mayo.

The vision and work came with confirmation after the lease, when asked to attend the District Conference of June, 2002, Presiding Elder, Rev. Floyd E. Chambers stated, "that there was not any available churches for pastorate and felt that I could start a society." At that time, building had already been leased and my response to Presiding Elder Chambers was, "You are a little too late, I **just** paid the lease ($500.00/month) on a building that day of his suggestion."

June 27, 2002, after minor renovations and additions, furniture was placed in building and Bible study was ongoing on Tuesday evenings at 6p.m. and Sunday Worship was only two Sundays a month. June 23, 2002, two souls were added to the church as candidates for baptism. The church started out with a membership of twelve, mostly family members.

On August 4, 2002, worship service began full time and five united and accepted Christ, saved, and Baptism Ceremony was performed by the late Rev. Curtis Brown, Pastor of St. Paul A.M.E. Zion Church at 505 South Union Street, Canton, Mississippi.

On October 26, 2002, under the Presiding Prelate, Bishop Nathaniel Jarrett, Missionary Supervisor, Mrs. Estelle Jarrett and Presiding Elder, Rev. Dr. Floyd E. Chambers, Jerusalem Temple was received into the African Methodist Episcopal Zion Church Connection.

December 29, 2002, another soul was added and baptized into Christ.

November 2, 2003, Jerusalem Temple was moved to 378 Goodloe Road, Canton, Mississippi, after Old Sims Chapel was vacant of pastorate Rev. Clora T. Handy. Rev. Chambers was compelled to offer the building as a monetary relief of lease at 5420 J. R. Lynch Street, Jackson, Mississippi Mississippi. Accepting the offer, the journey for Jerusalem Temple A.M.E. Zion Church at 5420 J. R. Lynch traveled to 378 Goodloe Road, Canton, Mississippi.

Many souls were added to the church. On October 22, 2004, Jerusalem Temple African Methodist Episcopal Zion Church at 378 Goodloe Road, Canton, Mississippi was officially, perpetually, named and Old Sims A.M.E. Zion Church name was void at the South Mississippi Annual Conference under the Presiding Prelate, Bishop Louis Hunter.

The church continued to grow both numerically and spiritually under the pastorate of Rev. Peggy V. McKenny. A new building was erected under Pastor Peggy V. McKenny and Presiding Elder Rev. Dr. Floyd E. Chambers and Presiding Prelate, Rev. Louis Hunter. Under the Presiding Prelate Bishop Darryl B. Starnes, A Dedication Ceremony was performed at the newly erected building in 2008.

October 24, 2010, Jerusalem Temple A.M.E. Zion Church received a new pastorate as Rev. Peggy V. McKenny, was compelled to seek new direction in ministry by the Holy Spirit. The pastoral charge was appointed to Rev. Joy Carrington Walker, by Bishop Darryl Starnes and Presiding Elder Gary D. Adams, Sr., Rev. Walker, after a few months relocated, and the charge was appointed to Rev. Sammy Brown, from St. Paul A.M.E. Zion Church, Canton Mississippi, who was initially recommended by Pastor Peggy McKenny, as led by the Holy Spirit, prior to moving forward from charge.

Rev. Sammy Brown continues to hold charge, as Pastor of Jerusalem Temple A.M.E. Zion Church, located at 378 Goodloe Road, Canton, Mississippi. Jerusalem Temple A.M.E. Zion Church is yet alive and doing well.

Humbly submitted,

Rev. Dr. Peggy V. McKenny, Ph.D. Theology
Pastor-Teacher of Greater Sims A.M.E. Zion Church
Organizer and Church planter, former pastor and teacher – Jerusalem Temple A.M.E. Zion Church.

Welcome to
THE CANTON PANOLA DISTRICT
REV. DR. FLOYD E. CHAMBERS, PRESIDES

The Canton-Panola District is spearheaded by the very capable and dynamic Rev. Dr. Floyd E. Chambers, lovingly referred to as the "Fiery Preacher" of the South Mississippi Conference.

He has been pastoring in the South Mississippi Conference for thirty years and has been the shepherd of the following flocks:

Free Chapel (1975-1979)
Walker Chapel (1975-1982)
Salem A.M.E .Zion Church (1979-1986)
Zion Chapel (1982-2006)
St. Paul A.M.E. Zion Church, Canton, Mississippi

He has served as Presiding Elder of the Meridian-Kosciusko and Canton-Panola District. He currently serves as Administrative Assistant for Bishop Mildred B. Hines.

As Presiding Elder, he currently oversees the following churches on the Canton-Panola District:

Greater Middleton Grove
Greater Murphy
Greater Salem
Liberty Hill
St. Paul (Cooksville)
St. Peter
Walker Chapel

GREATER SALEM AME ZION CHURCH

Telephone: 205-455-2574 ~ E-mail: greatersalemamez@yahoo.com

Post Office Box 164 ~ Panola, Alabama 35477

"Exemplifying God through: *Worship, Evangelism and Discipleship*"

Reverend Lelar Hodges-Brooks, Pastor

1950-1955

1976

Present

HISTORICAL SUMMARY OF THE GREATER SALEM AFRICAN METHODIST EPISCOPAL ZION CHURCH SALEM, ALAMBAMA 1895-2013

It has been said that a loss of history contributes to a loss of identity. Therefore, it is important to know, appreciate and respect the legacy of our church.

The history of Methodism in this country is generally conceded that its' light first shone forth in the city of New York in 1765. John Street Church, a white church, was the first Methodist Church in the city.

The white Methodists allowed Black people to attend their meetings but they imposed limitations and restrictions. These limitations included (1) they would license Black men to preach but they wouldn't ordain them. (2) Black people weren't permitted to take the Lord's Supper until all the White members had communed. (3) Black people were given a separate section in which to worship. And (4) in the absence of a White official, Black people were never to meet by themselves.

The stiff rules coming from the White Methodists were reprehensible to a certain New York group. After repeated insults, they decided that they could no longer endure the constant humiliation and restrictions imposed on them and this is the beginning of the African Methodist Episcopal Zion Church (A.M.E. Zion Church). The church was organized in 1796 and James Varick is credited with being the founder.

The African Methodist Episcopal Zion Church's position on slavery kept her out of the south for many years. It was Bishop Joseph J. Clinton who organized the A.M.E. Zion Church in the South.

The West Tennessee and Mississippi Conference was organized in Coffeeville, Mississippi in October 1869. The church had an abundant growth in the Delta area and the conference was very extensive; so the conference was divided into two portions by Bishop C.R. Harris at Meridian, Mississippi in December 1891. The Northern portion was from Memphis, Tennessee to Greenwood, Mississippi and retained the original name.

The Southern portion became known as the South Mississippi Conference and included an area from Yazoo City, Mississippi to Cooksville, Mississippi and Sherman, Alabama. At the time, this was a community located in Panola off County Road 83, also known as the Brockway Road. The Greater Salem A.M.E. Zion Church is included in the South Mississippi Conference. Although at one time, Salem wasn't the only church in Alabama that was a part of the South Mississippi Conference. St. Luke in Geiger was the other. Greater Salem was the only one to survive.

The Salem community is located in Sumter County, Alabama. The community fits into a fork by the Tombigbee and Noxubee Rivers. This site is also in the northern section of Sumter County near the Pickens County Line. Southeast of the town of Panola, Alabama, lies the proud community of Salem.

There were large plantations owned by White land owners and farmed by Black sharecroppers. The chief crops were cotton and corn. The Salem community produced its share. The sharecroppers paid their yearly rent to the plantation owners with cotton. Halves, thirds, and fourths were common terms for the sharecroppers. This cotton was taken to Panola, Alabama to the gin. Also, corn meal was produced in Panola for corn bread. The land and forest produced food that enabled the Black family to survive. Lights, freezers, and air conditioners were not heard of.

In the 1890's the Salem community realized that producing cotton and corn was essential for survival. However, salvation and eternal life were ingredients to becoming a total person. At this time, many Black families were attending the Shady Grove Methodist Church (White) of Panola, Alabama However, around the turn of the nineteenth century, these Black families became tired of having to sit in the balcony of the church, listening to the White minister tell them how to conduct themselves on the plantations. They were told how to work the land and treat the White plantation owners. Moreover, they were not allowed to participate in certain services in the church. Finally, Mr. Tom Stanton walked out. Mr. Lewis Bell, Mr. Wiley Little and others followed. With a vision to serve God as they pleased and wanting to know Him as their personal savior, they ventured out, and this led to the founding of the Greater Salem A.M.E. Zion Church.

The Black families of the community contacted the World Council of Churches and a representative came to the Tank (a train stop on the Ritter Place) to discuss the Black Methodist Doctrine. The families liked the word "African" in the A.M.E. Zion Church and how it could be associated with Black people.

The property of the Greater Salem A.M.E. Zion Church was purchased from Mr. C.M.A. Rogers for twenty dollars on the twelfth day of June in 1895. The deed was filed in the Probate Office of Sumter County on March 26, 1896 and recorded on May 15, 1896. This deed was later delivered to Mr. N. K. Smith on May 18, 1896.

Thank you Mr. Lewis Stanton, Mrs. Sarah Little, Mr. Pratt Speight, Mrs. Lou Speight, Mrs. Delphia Sanders, Mrs. Frances Stanton, Reverend Bush Stanton, Mrs. Classie Little, Mr. George Little, Mr. Tom Stanton, Mrs. Lee Anna Stanton, Mrs. Joanna Smith, Mr. William Smith, Mrs. Harriet Densmore, Mr. Eldred Densmore, and others, who, in 1895, built our first church, which was a log cabin type church near the gum tree where Mr. Flenoy Little's grave is now. The log cabin structure built by the founders and pioneers in 1895 was used until around 1914.

The early church was surrounded by a number of communities where the members lived on plantations. The following communities were associated with the church.

(1) The Ritter Place was located across the creek to the west of the church. The Densmores, Joneses, Speights, Smiths, and Dents lived there.

(2) The Stanton Quarter, where the Stantons lived, was located just back of the church. The Stantons included Rev. B. L. Stanton, Mr. Shephard, Sr., Mr. Barch, Mr. Joel, Mr. Nelson, Mr. Little, and Mr. Ulysses. In later years, Rev. Shephard, Jr., Mr. Bob, Mr. Onster, Mr. Toll, Mr. Clate, and Mr. Porter lived there.

(3) The Rogers Place was located southwest of the church where the Gholstons, Newtons, Smiths, Hendersons, Turners, Johnsons, Stantons, and Houstons lived.

(4) The Lauer-Bill Hill Community was located north of the church. The Jonses and Rogers lived there.

(5) Down the road, southeast of the church toward Gainsville, lived a large number of Littles, Daniels, Harsells, and Gholston.

(6) The Hampton Place was on the edge of the Noxubee River which was southeast of the church. The Littles, Thompkins, Gholstons, Grants, and Mornings lived there.

(7) The Morgan Place, located on the northeastern border of the Hampton Place was where the Childs, Gholstons, and Daniels lived.

(8) The Knight Place, where the Turners lived, was located east of the Morgan Place.

(9) The G-Ridge, east of the church, was where a number of members lived. This area included the Gholstons, the Belchars, and many others. These members could not attend church when weather was inclement.

This group of members, and members of other surrounding churches built or organized an extension of Greater Salem known as the Temple, where God could be served even during inclement weather. Mr. William Belchar, a member and officer of Greater Salem, was the Temple Leader. Mrs. Queen Gholston, presently a member of our church, experienced the Temple worship.

Now we can see how the church was surrounded by these nine plantations. Each plantation had a large number of Black families who worked the land and supported the Greater Salem Church. These families molded together for a very strong congregation.

Today, no one lives on the Ritter Place, the Rogers Place, the Morgan Place, the Lauer-Bill Hill, the Hampton Place, the Stanton Quarter, the Knight Place or the G-Ridge. However, Salem is still very strong in terms of dedicated members' enrollment and being spiritually and financially alive. Members now live in Panola, Geiger, Gainesville, Emelle, Boligee, Livingston, Eutaw, Tuscaloosa, and Birmingham, Alabama.

The second church was a frame church that younger families helped to build. Mr. Bob Little, Mr. Robert Smith, Mr. Hass Brown, Mr. Bill Little, and others built this structure. They moved the site from the gum trees to where the church stands today. The structure was remodeled around 1928 with the help of Mr. Willie Little, Sr., Mr. Shephard Stanton, Mr. William Belchar, Mr. George Little, and many others. However, this church was torn down in 1950.

The block church was the third building. It was started in 1950 and completed in 1955. The officers and members built the church themselves. The blueprint, materials, and labor were provided by members who included: Mr. Willie V. Little, Mr. Jessie Howard Little, Mr. Flenoy Little, Mr. Cleveland Gholston, Mr. Melvin Little, Reverend Jimmy Gholston, Mr. Dewey Little, Mr. Jlynn Dent, Mr. William S. Belchar and many other loyal officers and members who gave of themselves. While this structure was being built, services were held in the Salem School (previous home of the late Arthur and Charlotte Stanton).

In 1976, a plan was implemented to expand and renovate the existing block church. This expansion and renovation involved the decking of a new shingle top, the addition of a kitchen, and the addition of indoor-bathrooms. Later, renovations included a new floor with carpet, a new ceiling with insulation, new windows and doors, new church furniture including cushioned pews, brick around the exterior, central heat and air, a public address system, a new piano and organ, and a church bus. Other changes that occurred included the road in front of the church was paved, the cemetery had a face lift, and the church began to receive city water.

The year 2000 was the beginning of another chapter in the history of the Greater Salem A.M.E. Zion Church which included the construction of a completely new sanctuary and the remodeling of the old church building for classrooms, fellowship hall, etc. This building project was completed in 2001 and we can truly say that God is an awesome God for He has blessed us to have a beautiful new house of worship. And to God, we give all praises for the many blessings He has given to the Greater Salem African Methodist Episcopal Zion Church.

This present membership had a mixture of old and young officers working together for the advancement of the Church. Reverend Tracy Giles, Mr. Harzell Conway*, Mr. James Childs, Mr. David O. Jones, Mr. Felton Turner, Sr., Mr. Marshall Turner, Sr., Mr. Willie S. Little*, Mr. Albert Little*, Mr. Tommy C. Turner, Mr. Lawrence Conway, Mr. Faddis Little, and Mr. Porter Houston*. All of these persons are relatives of our founders and pioneers. (The * denotes that these individuals are deceased and are no longer with us).

This group of church leaders led the completion of the work started in 2000 in 2012. Trustees and Stewards include Mr. David O. Jones, Chairman, Mr. Rodger Morning, Vice Chairman, Mr. Lester Burrell, Secretary, Mr. Frank Maxwell, Treasurer, Mr. James Childs, Preacher Steward, Mr. Marshall Turner, Sr., Mr. Felton Turner, Sr., Mr. Leo Little, Mr. Gardner Howard, Mrs. Suzette Johnson, Mrs. Anita Dent, Mrs. Jones Little, Ms. Doris Gholston, Mr. Faddis Little, Mr. Frank Smith, and Mrs. Patricia Williams. Church leaders include Reverend Fred Brown, Pastor, Reverend Gary D. Adams, Presiding Elder, and the Rt. Reverend Darryl B. Starnes Presiding Bishop. The mortgage was scheduled to be completed in 2020. Thanks for doing an outstanding job for the advancement of God's kingdom. To God be the glory!

The Bible says where there is no vision, the people perish. Thanks to the founding fathers of the A.M.E. Zion Church and the Greater Salem A.M.E. Zion Church for having a vision of being able to freely worship and praise God without the White man looking over them or controlling them. Thanks to our current officers for their vision of a nice, spacious and comfortable church building for us today and for generations to come. And thanks to God Almighty for allowing Greater Salem to still be strong and one of the leading churches of the Canton-Panola District in the South Mississippi Conference of the African Methodist Episcopal Zion Church.

A full history of the Greater Salem A.M.E. Zion Church will never be known because sealed eternally are the lips of the early leaders who may not have been gifted in writing, or may have been hampered by other circumstance, such as not being given the opportunity to be open with their thoughts, and not being in a position to tell of deeds known. But, we know they dreamed dreams and looked to the future. Yes, dark days were there, but prayer and work enabled them to survive. And as we reflect upon our humble beginnings and as we celebrate our present accomplishments, let us never forget that it was God who brought us this far and let us humbly remember that only God can lead us on.

BISHOPS WHO PRESIDED OVER GREATER SALEM
1895-2013

Bishop Alstark	Bishop C. Coleman
Bishop Lee	Bishop R. L. Speaks
Bishop Woods	Bishop Alfred White
Bishop Spottswood	Bishop Nathaniel Jarrett
Bishop Joseph Johnson	Bishop Louis Hunter
Bishop C. Tucker	Bishop Darryl Starnes
	Bishop Mildred B. Hines

PRESIDING ELDERS WHO HELD QUARTERLIES AT GREATER SALEM
1895-2013

Elder J. R. Shepherd	Elder Faddis
Elder M. Mullin	Elder E. M. Boyd
Elder Tate	Elder C. W. Speights
Elder Blakley	Elder Curtis Brown
Elder Remant	Elder Harvest Wilkins
Elder Bennie Luckett	Elder Floyd Chambers
	Elder Gary Adams, Sr.
	Elder Floyd Chambers

MINISTERS WHO PASTORED GREATER SALEM
1895-2013

Reverend Dan Adams

Reverend L. Jackson

Reverend J. P. Marshall

Reverend Mitchell

Reverend N. S. Harris

Reverend T. L. Anderson

Reverend Jordan

Reverend W. L. Williams

Reverend C. C. White

Reverend Melone

Reverend R. M. Remant

Reverend Faddis

Reverend E. M. Boyd

Reverend Doshy

Reverend Harris

Reverend Horne

Reverend C. C. Craig

Reverend C. H. Beamon

Reverend James Ollie

Reverend Floyd Chambers

Rev. John Roberts

Reverend Hinton

Reverend J. H. Hilliard

Reverend J. S. Lott

Reverend Ed Miller

Reverend George Moore

Reverend Grosley

Reverend D. J.Garner

Reverend Andrew Beale

Reverend W. J. Neal

Reverend Robert Berry

Reverend W. J. Turner

Reverend Gary Adams, Sr.

Reverend Henry L. Brown

Reverend Tracy B. Giles

Reverend Moses Thompson

Reverend Terry White

Reverend Fred Brown

Reverend Lelar H. Brooks*

MINISTERS PRODUCED BY GREATER SALEM
1895-2013

Reverend Tony Harsell

Reverend Collin Gholston

Reverend John Little

Reverend Lucye Gholston

Reverend Jimmy Gholston

Reverend Willie Gholston

Reverend O. Little

Reverend Alexion Chaney

Reverend S. M. Stanton

Reverend Andrew Little

Reverend Charlie P. Little

Reverend Ransom Moore

Reverend Shannon Moore

Reverend Jethia H. Little

Reverend Sylvester Turner

Reverend Terrence Williams

PREACHER STEWARDS WHO SERVED GREATER SALEM
1895-2013

Mr. Tom Stanton

Mr. Bill Little

Mr. John Hinton

Mr. William S. Belchar

Mr. Dewey Little

Mr. George E. Turner

Mr. Jlynn Dent

Mr. James Childs

TRUSTEE CHAIRMEN WHO SERVED GREATER SALEM
1895-2013

Mr. Pratt Speight

Mr. Eldred Densmore

Mr. John Grant

Mr. Flenoy Little

Mr. Jimmy Gholston

Mr. Willie V. Little

Mr. David O. Jones

Mr. Fred L. Woods

Mr. Harzell Conway, Jr.

Mr. David O. Jones

SUNDAY SCHOOL SUPERINTENDENTS WHO SERVED GREATERSALEM
1895-2013

Mr. Miller Speight	Mr. L. Newton
Reverend J. T. Little	Mr. Melvin Little
Mr. Flenoy Little	Reverend S.M. Stanton
Mr. John Hinton	Mr. Lawrence Conway
Rev. Andrew Little	Mrs. Ola Houston.

Left:
Rev. Floyd Chambers prepares for
The wedding.

Right: Rev. Floyd Chambers performs
the wedding. Groom, Albert & wife
"jump the broom" during the ceremony.

Mine Eyes Have Seen the Glory

Battle Hymn of the Republic
Julia Ward How and William Steffe

Mine eyes have seen the glory of the coming of the Lord
He is tramping out the vintage where the grapes of wrath are stored
He has loosed the faithful lightening of His terrible swift sword
His truth is marching on

I have seen Him in the watch fires of a hundred circling camps
They have builded Him an altar in the evening dews and damps
I can read His righteous sentence by the dim and glaring lamps
His day is marching on

He has sounded forth the trumpet that shall never call retreat
He is sifting out the hearts of men before the judgment seat
O be swift my soul to answer Him be jubilant my feet
Our God is marching on

In the beauty of the lilies Christ was born across the sea
With a glory in His Bosom that transfigures you and me
As He died to make men holy, let us die to make men free
While God keeps marching on

Glory, Glory, Hallelujah
Glory, Glory, Hallelujah
Glory, Glory, Hallelujah
His truth is marching on.

ZION CHAPEL AME ZION CHURCH HISTORY-1874-2013
PASTOR: Rev. Gary D. Adams, Sr.

Zion Chapel African Methodist Episcopal Zion Church had its beginning about one half mile south of its present location. There are markers, including a cemetery, denoting its initial location. After many years in its beginning location, Zion Chapel moved its small membership to its present site using a lodge hall which was the society hall, to hold service.

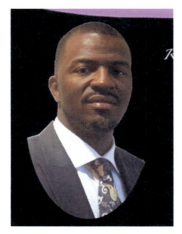

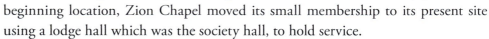

In 1874, the first church was built where the church now stands, six miles east of Canton, off Robinson Road. With constant efforts and prayers, the church also became a classroom with Mrs. Florence Jones as the teacher. This educational endeavor continued until the building was completely destroyed by fire in late 1915. A smaller church was rebuilt. The trustees at that time were Bros: John Levy Lane, Jeff Jones, Harrison Carter, Tom Luckett, Harper Brooks, Hercules Jones, Sr., and Miles Love.

Zion Chapel saw many prospering years of growth. Then in 1926, the church was destroyed by lightening. The structure was rebuilt and Zion Chapel continued to grow both spiritually and financially. Rev. John Hilliard was the pastor. The trustees at this time were Bros: Jerry Sanders, Willie Burrell, Sr., Anderson Roberts, Sam Jones, Johnny Johnson, Marsh Blackmon, Willie Brooks, Sr., and Jessie Jackson, Jr. Mr. Freeman Johnson was the contractor.

In 1961 a new structure was built because of the present building being in such poor condition. Rev. John Roberts was the pastor. Trustees were Bros: Prince Roberts, Willie Brooks, Henry Brooks, Harry Luckett, Zeb Green, Otha Lyles, Webster Brown, Claude Roberts, Sr., and Hercules Towner, Sr., Mr. Robert Beamon was the contractor.

In 1986 Zion Chapel, under the pastorate of Rev. Floyd E. Chambers built a new sanctuary. The church and its members saw a vision for the future that included expanding for future growth. Trustees were Bros: William Watts, Harris J. Roberts, Alex Sutton, Peyton Baker, Jr. Wallace Green, and Hercules Jones, who was also the contractor.

After several years, Zion Chapel added a fellowship hall, a kitchen, classrooms, and a conference room on the east side of the church. Since the addition, Zion Chapel has hosted numerous annual conferences and ensures that the church is always available and utilized for other church related activities.

In 2001 Zion Chapel was blessed once again to enter a new sanctuary that seats 300 comfortably. Bro. William Watts saw this new project take shape and worked faithfully until his health failed. Therefore, the Fellowship Hall was named in his honor. Trustees were Vicence Brown, Chairman, Arthur Brooks, Wallace Green, Clarence Reed, Dewayne Sutton, Bartholomus Glass, Frazier Jones, Sam Handy, Timothy Chambers, Edgar Hunt, and Edward Lindsey. James Patrick Burks, Vann Towner, Vicence Brown, and Charles Luckett were the primary contractors for the project, however, the entire church family worked diligently to ensure that the work was completed in a timely manner.

Zion Chapel envisions the strengthening of its community ties through educational programs for children, youth and adults. It is anticipated that through community based programs this can be facilitated.

Zion Chapel A.M.E. Zion Church has through the years, literally been through the fire, storm and the rain, but thanks to God, the church and its members are moving forward with God at the helm.

The Lewis School: The Lewis School was the first in the Robinson Road community. This school housed first through eighth grade. It also served as the Willing Workers Society Hall. In 1915, Zion Chapel A.M.E. Zion Church burned to the ground. At this time church services were held in the Lewis School. Today, the school has been named as a historical location in Madison County.

Ministers:	Presiding Elders:	Bishops:	
Rev. Benjamin	Rev. Ben Williams	Rev. W. L. Lee	1916-1927
Rev. Baldwin	Rev. Banks	Rev. J. W. Ward	1920-1940.
Rev, John Hilliard	Rev. D. S. Williams	Rev. B. F. Gordon	1944-1952
Rev. I. L. C. Robinson	Rev. Dan Adams	Rev. S. G. Spottswood	1952-1956
Rev. Mirack	Rev. L. H. McMullin	Rev. C. E. Tucker	1956-1972
Rev. C. A. Steed	Rev. Jimmie C. Hicks	Rev. C. R. Coleman	1972-1980
Rev. Owens	Rev. Bennie Luckett	Rev. Reuben Speaks	1980-1984
Rev. C. C. Speights	Rev. Floyd Chambers	Rev. Alfred White	1984-1992
Rev. Clarence Goodloe	Rev. Gary D. Adams, Sr.	Rev. Joseph Johnson	1992-1996
Rev. John Roberts		Rev. Nathaniel Jarrett	1996-2004
Rev. Andrew Griffin		Rev. Louis Hunter	2004-2008
Rev. W. T. Hawthorne		Rev. Darryl Starnes	2008-2012
Rev. Rev. James Ollie		Rev. Mildred B. Hines	2012-Present
Rev. Floyd Chambers			
Rev. Gary D. Adams, Sr.			

MARCHING UPWARD TO ZION

"Come ye that love the Lord, and let your joys be known; join in a song of sweet accord, join in a song of sweet accord; and thus surround the throne, and thus surround the throne. We're marching to Zion, beautiful, beautiful Zion. We're marching upward to Zion, that beautiful City of God."

Rev. Floyd Chambers

VBS Mrs. Hattie Chambers-Christian Ed Teacher

Right - VBS: Ms. Clova Burks, teacher

VBS Christian Ed Class

Terwinda Banks

Buds of Promise

Honoring Elders

VBS – Mrs. Hurtistene Watts-teacher

VBS – Mrs. Dannie Jones –teacher-(lt-in hat)   Church picnic Ms Lucille Williams, front

Left: Rev. Bonnie Travis provides watermelon treat at VBS

Christmas Play

Mr. Harris Judge Roberts

Choir Day

Hurtistene Watts (lt) Eunice Hicks
(center) & Hattie Chambers (rt)

Church retreat

Women's Day

**ZC celebrates African
American History Month**

Male Choir

Ms Mazalene Towner, center

Right: Elder Women: Ms Dannie Jones, Ms Bettie Nash & Ms Lucille Williams

Women's praise dance Team

Men's praise dance team

GREATER MURPHY AME ZION –LATE 1800'S-2013
2260 Loring Road -Camden, Mississippi
PASTOR: REV. CHARLES BROWN

Murphy Chapel A.M.E. Zion Church, was organized in the late 1800's on donated land. The church was rebuilt in 1928 with the following trustees making an impact: W.M. Simpson, Zinkie Martin, Will Collins, Clark Oliver, John Olive, W.M. Hamblin, Lidge Walker, Amos Heath and Harvey Parker.

Mrs. Carobel Milton Chapman, an elementary teacher, and her niece, Elise Hodo, legally and officially conveyed to Murphy's Chapel Church 4.25 acres, which includes the cemetery, on March 14, 1980. The following trustees were referenced as grantees: Randolph Brown, Leon Stokes, Elton Flax, David Lee Brown, Ollie Williams, Lee Singleton, Helen Sutherland, Lillie Williams and E.C. Ollie.

Left of the church stood the silver bell. The bell was used on Sunday mornings, at funerals to notify members of the approaching hearses, and in emergencies when all the town residents needed to gather for meetings. It was removed during construction. It currently rests about two miles from the church and anxiously awaits resurrection. The white wood frame church, with the steep steps did not have bathrooms or air conditioning; and additions were not made until the early 1960's when Rev. Bennie Luckett became pastor. In 1985, the members decided to build a new church. It was erected on the hill.

After the completion, Sunday school and worship services were held every Sunday. Previous years services were held only twice a month. ***The pastors*** who have served at Murphy Chapel Church date to about 1928. Rev. Bennie and Mrs Marcella Luckett were the longest serving. Rev. Lelar H. Brooks was the first female pastor serving from October 2006 to October 2012. Rev. Charles and Mrs. Angela Brown were appointed in October 2012 and currently serve.

The trustees at the helm since 2006 or later are: Tonya Parker, Percy Catchings, Jr., Helen Parker, Alfred Boyd, Sr., Eunice White, Nola White, Maggie Catchings, Albert Scott, Dwight Vaughn, Mac Luckett and Gloria Smith. Alfred Boyd, Sr., later followed his call to go into the ministry and would no longer serve.

The Board of Stewards consist of: Michelle Vaughn, Percy Catchings, Sr., Doris Smith, Bettye Boyd, Fred

Tucker, Odell White, Chris Evans and Janice Olive. There are so many who had a major impact on the growth of the church like Randolph Brown.

The current ministerial staff includes: Rev. Jackie Johnson, Sister Cassandra Jackson, Bro. Alfred Boyd, Sr., Sister Diane Young and Sister Nancy Bennett.

Under Rev. Luckett's leadership, the present building was built in 1985. The new church, Greater Murphy, had a new name and a new motto, "The Church where Everybody is Somebody." Ollie Williams and Percy Catchings, Sr., were preacher stewards during his tenure. Rev. Bennie Luckett was a pioneer for *"Miles Traveled, Doors Opened, and Lives Touched," and* for forty-eight years he served Greater Murphy and a community of folk. A special Canton-Panola District appreciation orchestrated by Pastor Charles Brown, in honor of Rev. Luckett's forty eight year achievement was held on April 21, 2013 at Greater Murphy. History was once again made, as proclaimed by Madison County and Supervisor, Paul E. Griffin, that April 21, 2013 was Rev. Bennie Luckett day.

Trustees appointed during Rev. Luckett's tenure were: Leon Stokes, Albert Scott, Lee Singleton; Marcella Luckett, Lille Williams, Annie Brown, E. C. Ollie, Daniel Brown, L. C. Dawson and Curtis Evans, Sr. Presiding Elder was Rev. Dr. Jimmie C. Hicks and the Bishop was Reuben L. Speaks and later would be Bishop Nathaniel Jarrett.

More recent improvements began as Phase 1, shortly after Rev. Lelar Brooks was appointed in 2006. Improvements included renovations to the foyer, restrooms, and a complete overhaul to the sanctuary as well as electrical and heating upgrades in 2007. Flower beds and other outdoor grooming was completed in June of 2009. Grave yard clean-up day was also a part of the history of Murphy Chapel's and was formed to improve the care of the grounds. Therefore, it served as a day of fellowship for the members and community coming together in unity. Before long, the observance was yearly with food "on the grounds," being provided by the women. On June 27, 2009, graveyard clean-up day was re-birthed.

A parsonage and Head Start school building were located on the south side of the road in front of the church.

The parsonage was used for pastors although not many lived there. When it was no longer used for pastors, many families, the Gus Reed family, the Ward Family and others, lived in the home until about the 1980's. It was torn down and now serves as a mini park area for church picnics. The cemetery is located on the north side, west of the church and now extends farther westward.

The present membership includes many of the descendants of the original trustees. The oldest living members as of 2013 are Clementine Dawson and Albert Scott. There are a total of fourteen class leaders with two hundred-three members. Greater Murphy has seen tremendous growth since Pastor Charles Brown's appointment in October 2012. In fact the first ever "worship in the park" family and friends was held with a picnic after services on September 1, 2013 with over three hundred people waiting to hear the Word. Currently we have witnessed a lot of "firsts." Pastor Brown always salutes those who have labored faithfully before him and praises God for the foundation they laid.

Currently Presiding Prelate is female, Bishop Mildred B. Hines, and the current Presiding Elder is, Rev. Dr. Floyd E. Chambers who presides under the umbrella of a third District, Canton-Panola.

The other two districts are Canton-Sharon and Jackson-Gallman. From 1958 to present day, August, 30, 2013, there have been only three pastors to shepherd Greater Murphy African Methodist Episcopal Zion Church.

Pastors:
Rev. Parstell, Rev. Wade Hampton, Rev. Golf, Rev. Edward D. Miller, Rev. W. T. Hawthorne, Rev. Bennie Luckett, Rev .Lelar H .Brooks, and Rev. Charles Brown.

Bishops:
Bishop Mildred B. Hines, current: Bishop, Bishop Darryl B. Starnes, Sr., Bishop Louis Hunter, Bishop Nathaniel Jarrett.

Elders:
Rev. D. S. Williams, Rev. Jimmie C. Hicks, Rev. Floyd E. Chambers, Rev. Gary D. Adams, Sr., Rev. Floyd E. Chambers

Trustees:
W. M. Simpson, Zinkie Martin, Will Collins, Clark Oliver, John Olive, W. M. Hamblin, Lidge Walker, Amos Heath and Harvey Parker,

Randolph Brown, Leon Stokes, Eton Flax, David Lee Brown, Ollie Williams, lee Singleton, Helen Sutherland, Lillie Williams, E.C. Ollie, Annie B. Brown, Daniel Brown, L. C. Dawson and Curtis Evans, Sr.

Tonya Parker, current President, Percy Catchings, Jr., Helen Parker, Alfred Boyd, Sr., Eunice White, Nola White, Maggie Catchings, Albert Scott, Dwight Vaughn, Mac Luckett and Gloria Smith. Alfred Boyd, Sr., who later followed his call to go into the ministry and would no longer serve.

Stewards:
Michelle Vaughn, current Preacher Stewardess, Percy Catchings, Sr., Doris Smith, Bettye Boyd, Fred Tucker, Odell White, Christopher Evans and Janice Olive.

Deaconess:
Bettye Boyd, President, Rosie Boyd, Clemmie Dawson, Minnie Martin, Lola Ward, Fannie Gordon, Alice Holmes (died on 10/1/13), Lizzie Vaughn, Elnora Evans, Mary Crawford, and Eunice White.

Sunday school Superintendents:

Elton Flax, Leon Stokes, Timothy Luckett, Tonya Parker, Helen Parker, current superintendent

Ministers:

Rev. Jackie Johnson, Sis. Casandra C. Jackson, Bro. Alfred Boyd, Sr., Sister Nancy Bennett and Sister Diane Young

Conference Workers:

Faye Vaughn, and Brenda Nettles

2009 was the first attempt to compile such a document for the family and friends Souvenir Booklet. Thanks to Rev. Bennie & Mrs. Marcella Luckett, Mrs. Rosie Boyd and Mr. John White, ll, of Chicago, Illinois for their input. To date, no other records exist to our knowledge.

GREATER MIDDLETON GROVE AFRICAN METHODIST EPISCOPAL ZION CHURCH – 1820-2013

PASTOR: Rev. Moses Thompson

Greater Middleton Grove African Methodist Episcopal Zion Church is located in Madison County, Mississippi at 602 Way Road, Canton.

About 1820, one acre of land was donated by John Middleton to Middleton Grove A.M.E. Zion Church. At that time a little wooden church facing the north and south was built on the land.

No history of this church could be found from 1820 to 1944.

Rev. W. T. Hawthorne was appointed to serve as pastor of Middleton Grove, in 1944 and served a total of thirty-four years. During his tenure, Rev. Hawthorne was transferred to the West Alabama Conference and Rev. Dan McKay served two years as pastor of Middleton Grove. Rev. Hawthorne was reappointed to Middleton Grove and served until he retired in 1980. Under Rev. Hawthorne and Rev. McKay, worship service was only held on the first and third Sundays of each month. Holy Communion was always on the first Sunday as it is currently.

Middleton Grove was rebuilt in 1963. The church was re-built facing east and west in direction. Roosevelt Brown served as Chairman of the Trustee Board. Other trustees included Henry Nichols, Curtis Brown, Walter L. Small, Lee Banks, Mac Owens, A. C. Chambers, Vera Collins and Benjamin "Joe" Small. Rev. W. T. Hawthorne was the pastor. At that time, Middleton Grove was on the Canton-Jackson District.

Rev. Willie C. Cable was appointed as pastor in 1980, and served until 1987. During Rev. Cable's tenure, the fellowship hall was added to the church.

Rev. Andre D. Grant was appointed pastor and served for seventeen years, November 1987 to April 2004. During this time, Middleton Grove began having worship service every Sunday.

In 1992 the A.M.E. Zion Episcopal districts were previously identified by numbers but in 1992 we were given the name "Southwestern Delta Episcopal District." Also in 1992, Middleton Grove was assigned to the Meridian-Kosciusko-Laurel District. Under Rev. Grant's leadership, Middleton Grove officially adopted the name Greater Middleton Grove when it was remodeled, and the church was also bricked in 1993. At that time, trustees were Spencer Harries, Vanessa Van, Mary Brown, Vera Collins, Precious Brown, Raymond Sykes, Earl Johnson, Bruce Brown and Fitzgerald Small, Chairman. Under his leadership, a church van was also purchased.

In 1995, Laurel was dropped from the District name. Greater Middleton Grove remained a part of the Meridian-Kosciusko District.

From April 2004 to October 2006, Rev. Lelar Brooks was appointed as Pastor.

In 2006, the Meridian-Kosciusko District's name was changed to the Canton-Panola District.

In October 2006, Rev. Moses E. Thompson was appointed as pastor. During Pastor Thompson's first year,

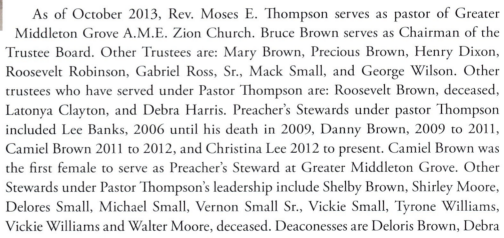

the church van was traded for a new van, which was paid in full at the time of purchase. About a year later, about 2008, the church financed a second van. The church completed payments for the second van in 2011. The church now owns two vans, both paid in full.

In March 2011, Greater Middleton Grove published its first newsletter. The newsletter is distributed on the first Sunday of each month in the church, community, and via e-mail.

As of October 2013, Rev. Moses E. Thompson serves as pastor of Greater Middleton Grove A.M.E. Zion Church. Bruce Brown serves as Chairman of the Trustee Board. Other Trustees are: Mary Brown, Precious Brown, Henry Dixon, Roosevelt Robinson, Gabriel Ross, Sr., Mack Small, and George Wilson. Other trustees who have served under Pastor Thompson are: Roosevelt Brown, deceased, Latonya Clayton, and Debra Harris. Preacher's Stewards under pastor Thompson included Lee Banks, 2006 until his death in 2009, Danny Brown, 2009 to 2011, Camiel Brown 2011 to 2012, and Christina Lee 2012 to present. Camiel Brown was the first female to serve as Preacher's Steward at Greater Middleton Grove. Other Stewards under Pastor Thompson's leadership include Shelby Brown, Shirley Moore, Delores Small, Michael Small, Vernon Small Sr., Vickie Small, Tyrone Williams, Vickie Williams and Walter Moore, deceased. Deaconesses are Deloris Brown, Debra Harris, Hattie Owens, Annie Pearl Small, Carolyn Small and Delores Small.

Dates are unknown, however, those who have served as church secretary are as followed consecutively Sylvia Hewitt, Catherine Small, Hattie Brown, Linda Brown, Lorraine Johnson, and Camiel Brown.

Presiding Prelates have included:

- 1948 – 1956 Bishop Stephen S. Spottswood
- 1956 -1972 Bishop Charles Eubanks Tucker
- 1972-1980 Bishop Clinton R. Coleman
- 1980 – 1988 Bishop Rueben L. Speaks
- 1988 -1992 Bishop Alfred E. White
- 1992 – 1996 Bishop Joseph Johnson
- 1996 – 2004 Bishop Nathaniel Jarrett
- 2004 – 2008 Bishop Louis Hunter
- 2008 – 2012 Bishop Darryl B. Starnes
- 2012 – Bishop Mildred B. Hines, first female bishop

Presiding Elders have included:

- Circa 1940's Rev. Dan. Adams
- Circa 1956 – 1972 Rev. D. S. Williams
- 1972 – 1975 Rev. Samuel Martin Taylor
- 1975 – 1993 Rev. Jimmie C. Hicks
- 1993 – 2001 Rev. Bennie Luckett
- 2001 – 2008 Rev. Floyd E. Chambers
- 2008 – December 2012 Rev. Gary D. Adams, Sr.
- December 2012 present Rev. Dr. Floyd E. Chambers

Please accept this Middleton Grove A.M.E. Zion Church History to the 123rd South Mississippi Annual Conference. A Copy will be placed in the church archives.

Humbly Submitted on this 10th day of October 2013.

Rev. Moses E. Thompson, Pastor

Bruce Brown, Chairman of Trustees

Christina Lee, Preacher's Steward

Camiel Brown, Church Secretary

Presiding Elder D. S. Williams and Rev. Hawthorne at Middleton Grove

left-right: Rev. Lelar Brooks, Rev. Bonnie Travis, Rev. Andre Grant, Rev. Moses Thompson, and Presiding Elder John C. Evans, Jr. at Greater Middleton Grove

ST. PETER AME ZION CHURCH
1880-2013
"Looking Back…Reaching Forward"

Pastor: REVEREND OLA DIXON

St. Peter started out as a small building close to a section called "Brown's Quarter." A Reverend Powell, whose initials are not known, was founder of the Zion Church in Meridian. He was known to be an "exciting preacher," one having deep convictions and great zeal for the church and cause of Christ.

Brown's Quarter was the site of this African Methodist Episcopal Zion Church in the year of 1880. Some years later this congregation moved to 1322 36th Street, Meridian, Mississippi. From there the church moved to its current location.

The church has gone through many metamorphic changes over the years. The original structure was a very beautiful wooden structure erected by Rev. L. S. Jones between 1880 and 1882. However, as the years passed, this building continued to deteriorate although still somewhat desirable. After much debate and planning, the future of this structure was decided, despite firm opposition by the presiding elder at that time. This structure was eventually torn down and rebuilt. Under the leadership of Rev. W.H. Alexander, this edifice was razed and rebuilt, much less attractively. Rev. Alexander served the church for seven years.

After Rev. Alexander's departure, the church became spiritually weak. During the leadership of Rev. Reed, his successor, that the new building was destroyed by a mysterious fire. During this era many ministers came and left, and for a long time the congregation had no adequate place to worship. There were times when the parsonage was used for worship services and at other times services were conducted under an arbor like shelter stretched over the ruins left by the first church. There was an even greater exodus of members during that time. Many of the most influential members of the congregation were included in this group.

The spiritual and physical decline of the church continued for a number of years. It was not until Rev. J. W. Bennett, arrived that renewed attention was given to constructing a stable place for worship. It was under his leadership that plans were begun to properly house this congregation in 1947. With the help of the Zion connection, members and friends, the erection of a third church was begun. Unfortunately, Rev. Bennett was replaced as pastor due to failing health, prior to completion of the work. He was replaced by Rev. Paul A. Silas at the next Annual Conference. However, Rev. Silas was unable to move forward with the completion of the building.

In December of 1951, Rev. A. C. Pait from the Michigan Conference was appointed pastor. Rev. Pait was credited for successful completion of this structure and a second cornerstone was laid and inscribed as follows:

St. Peter A.M. E. Zion Church
Rebuilt December 1947
B.F. Gordon – Bishop
W. J. Bennett – Pastor
W. B. Faddis – Presiding Elder

TRUSTEES:
Isaiah Payne, Chairman
Sam Rembert, Treasurer
John W. Larkin, Secretary
Leon Kendrick
L. B. O'Bannon
Nero Roberts

IN MEMORY OF:
Rev. Alton Pait, P.E.
Departed – January 7, 1956

By the time of his death in 1956, Rev. Pait was credited with building several Zion Churches in the South.

In 1956, after Rev. Pait's death, his wife who was also a minister, was given the charge. She served as pastor for about a year, but, because of the demands of the job, she decided to return to her native home in Detroit where she could better serve the church.

In 1957, Rev. McClain was appointed pastor to St. Peter and served for a short time. Rev. Lillian Brunner succeeded Rev. McClain. She had a magnetic personality which led to increasing membership by encouraging members to become workers for Christ. Under the leadership of Rev. Brunner, the church was renovated and a second parsonage was purchased. Rev. Brunner was later transferred to the New York Conference.

Once again, St. Peter was without a pastor for several months. During this time Bishop Tucker came to St. Peter one Sunday a month. Finally, after sometime, Rev. McGee was appointed as pastor and served this congregation for two years, followed by Rev. McCay. It is unclear how long he served.

In 1967, Rev. Craig was sent to St. Peter and served for an undocumented length of time, followed by Rev. C. W. Speights, who served as pastor for six years.

In 1974, Bishop Clinton R. Coleman sent Rev. W. T. Hawthorne to pastor the church. He served for twenty months. Once again the church was left without a pastor, also without a place of worship. We were then worshipping in the Good Shepherd Lutheran Church in the afternoon on the second and fourth Sundays of each month. The membership was restless and worn. A few members stayed together and prayed for a brighter day. During this period, these members served in the capacity of Trustees: E.L. Fluker, Jr., William Chaney, Billie Alexander, Sebelle Willis, Theola Hayes Fluker, and O. R. Washington.

In November of 1976, Bishop Clinton R. Coleman appointed Reverend J. P. Phillips to St. Peter. Under the auspices of Reverend J. P. Phillips, the updating of the record keeping and various treasurers brought about much frustration and confusion in the church

Reverend Phillips came to St. Peter young in the ministry, and facing conditions that had existed for many years. He was faced with a difficult task of bringing the people together and providing a place of worship.

With the help of God and the willingness of Reverend Phillips, the move was made. With the help of the Trustees, Mr. E. L. Fluker, perhaps the most outstanding, and a highly influential officer, he was a faithful, warmhearted servant of the church. He was a successful master planner, and his work carried him to many places.

It was under Reverend J. P. Phillips' guidance, the transition from idea into reality was accomplished, and on November 22, 1977, the Eighty Seventh Session of the South Mississippi Conference of the A.M.E. Zion Church opened at 10:30 a.m. in the new St. Peter A.M.E. Zion Church on this site. Reverend Phillips served this congregation from 1976 to the mid 80's. In 1992, Rev. Robert Chambliss spearheaded renovations of the existing building. A new dining room, kitchen and office space was added.

PASTORS OF ST. PETER:
Reverend Messrs, Stokes, Green and Johnson, whose dates of service are unknown. A Reverend Jones served the Congregation while it worshipped in a small, one-room "shot-gun" building on the lot that is now numbered 1320 36th Avenue. A Reverend Hall succeeded Rev. Jones. Other pastors were the Reverends Hamilton, Hill, Blackledge, Henderson, Byrd, Lewis, Cost, Stanton, Byrd, Alexander, Reed, Young, Marshall, Larkin, Prince, Harper, Sanders, Jackman, Gaylord, Rice, Singleton, Williamson, Glover, Berry, Grant,

For the lines are fallen unto me on pleasant places, yea, I have a goodly inheritance.

Psalm 16:16

LIBERTY HILL AME ZION CHURCH
50 Attala Street, Durant, MS 39063
724 Cedar Street
1974 – 2005
2005 – Present

Liberty Hill started with the Bruce Foundation which consisted of the Bruce, Culp, McGee and Davis families. The year is not known of origin, but Liberty Hill was originally located out in the rural area of Holmes County, with Rev. John Williams serving as the pastor. Mr. John Davis and Mr. Jake McGee Sr. were the Stewards and Mrs. Mattie Foster, serving as the secretary.

After the death of Mrs. Mattie Foster, Mrs. Louise Bruce served as secretary until her death in 1992. Her daughter, Martha Bruce served for a few months and Mrs. Shirley Frizell-Fletcher began to serve, and has served until this present time.

During the tenure of Rev. Curtis Brown, in April, 1974, Liberty Hill was moved from the rural area to its present location, 724 Cedar Street. Mr. Walter Bruce Jr. was the contractor and the chairman of the trustee board. Other members of the trustee board were Mr. Nathan Bruce, Mr. Jake McGee, Sr., Mr. Leotha Patterson, and Mr. John H. Brown.

Rev. W. M. Stevenson, Worship Master of Martin Lodge #170, laid the cornerstone, with Rev. S. M. Taylor serving the Meridian/Kosciusko District as the Presiding Elder. They did not just leave the land in the rural area without the generations knowing where they started; the land of the old church is now "Liberty Hill African Methodist Episcopal Zion Church

Cemetery." Many have come and many have gone, but never forgotten. Liberty Hill has come a long way since the days of that rural church, with many steps crossing the threshold of those doors.

Under the present pastorate, Rev. Bonnie Travis, Liberty Hill has made many strives, one being the construction of a new sanctuary. Bishop Louis Hunter was serving South Mississippi Annual Conference and Rev. Floyd Chambers, Presiding Elder. Stewards: Mr. Walter Bruce, Lillian Johnson, Curtis Jones, Alvin Sims and Kendrick Collins. Trustees: Bo Patterson, Larry Zollicoffer, Gregory Potee, Torry Potee, and Warren Hallmon.

LIBERTY HILL A.M.E. ZION CHURCH
Celebrate the Installation of their Cornerstone

Pictured from L to R: Jimmie Brooks, Master of Billingslea Lodge 367-A in Goodman, Rev. Bonnie R. Travis, Pastor, Liberty Hill, The Right Rev. Darryl B. Starnes, Bishop of the South Mississippi Annual Conference, and Rev. Gary D. Adams, Sr., Presiding Elder of the Canton-Panola District

The Liberty Hill African Methodist Episcopal Zion Church of Durant was rebuilt in 2005, and on April 22, 2012, Billingslea Masonic Lodge 367-A PHA, installed the Cornerstone, with the services led by The Right Rev. Darryl B. Starnes, Bishop of the South Miss Annual Conference, Southwestern Delta Episcopal Area and President of the board of Bishops of the African Methodist Episcopal Zion Church. He was assisted by Rev. Gary D. Adams, Sr., Presiding Elder of the Canton/Panola District, Rev. Bonnie Travis, Pastor of Liberty Hill, and other ministers and pastors of the Conference. Left, **Standing: Rev. Earnestine Sims, Rev. Manuel James and Rev. Acquanette Johnson. Sitting: Pastor, Rev. Bonnie Travis**

Rev. Bonnie Travis

Baptism in pool

Marching for Freedom

PASTORS
Rev. John Williams
Rev. C. Craig
Rev. Leon Anderson
Rev. Curtis Brown
Rev. Vaughn Burke
Rev. Herman Coleman
Rev. Paul Lee
Rev. Bonnie Travis

PRESIDING ELDERS
Rev. S. M. Taylor
Rev. Bennie Luckett
Rev. Floyd Chambers
Rev. Gary Adams
Rev. Wilkerson
Rev. Bennie Luckett
Rev. Floyd E. Chambers
Rev. Jimmie C. Hicks
Rev. Gary Adams

<u>BISHOPS</u>:

The Bishops who served this conference of Zion were the Bishop J. B. Alstark, Petty, Lee, J. W. Woods, B. G. Shaw, B. F. Gordon, J. C. Taylor, S. G. Spottswood, C. E. Tucker, Bishop Clinton R. Coleman, Rueben L. Speaks, Alfred White, Joseph Johnson, Nathaniel Jarrett, Bishop Louis Hunter, Bishop Darryl Starnes and Bishop Mildred B. Hines.

Compiled and written from information provided by some of the current members
dating back to the 1935-1940's and the late Sis. Alice Elaine Johnson.

THE STORY OF WALKER CHAPEL AME ZION CHURCH
1923-2013
PASTOR: Rev. Isabel Scott

The church we know as Walker Chapel was first organized in 1921. Its arrangers were the late Mr. and Mrs. Lewis Walker, Rev. Lally and several other members.

In 1923, the late Mr. and Mrs. Lewis Walker sold and deeded a parcel of land where the church now stands, to the African Methodist Episcopal Zion Conference for the purpose of erecting a church on it. The construction of the church was initiated. Lewis Walker, whose name the church bears, was unable to assist with the building of the church because he was disabled: However he had a strong desire to do so. His words from his sick bed were, "If I was only able, I would build that church"!

The original trustees of the church were E. G. Cunningham, Ernest Marshall and J. W. Morgan.

Several years after the church was established, it was destroyed by fire. The faithful members did not give up; they held services in their homes until the church was rebuilt.

Approximately 1950 or 1951, the church suffered a severe blow. It was partially destroyed by a windstorm. It was rebuilt under the leadership of Rev. S. S. Brunner.

Walker Chapel A.M.E. Zion Church is a member of the Canton-Panola District of the South Mississippi Conference under the leadership of Bishop Mildred B. Hines. Our Presiding Elder is Rev. Dr. Floyd Chambers. Rev. Chambers was Pastor of Walker Chapel from 1976 until 1992.

Rev. Rebecca Gross was appointed after Rev. Chambers. She was a faithful woman of God full of joy and outgoing. She would always say, "God is real, stop playing church, and, let the anointing fall on us, Saints." The church was in poor condition and needed many repairs. But through it all, God made a way. Rev. Gross was a remarkable pastor, teacher and a mother hen. She would go out of her way and would give you her last dime. She didn't let anything shake her faith and kept on preaching, like nothing was wrong. Rev. Gross remained at Walker Chapel until she retired.

After Rev. Gross retired, Rev. Clifton Granger became Pastor. He was an outstanding speaker. He would visit the sick and go around the community telling people about Jesus Christ. The members worked together improving the church. They even spent their own money. There were many gospel programs held to raise money for the church. Rev. Granger was Pastor of Walker Chapel for three years.

Rev. Michael Chapman was appointed Pastor of Walker Chapel in 1996 as an ordained Deacon. He was ordained Elder in 1998. His motto was:

"At Walker Chapel A.M.E. Zion Church, we do things God's Way!" Rev. Chapman was a good listener. He was a man with his own style. He saw things and drew a blue print in his mind how God gave it to him. One Sunday morning, he preached "Do you see what I see God's Vision." Rev. Chapman said God gave him a dream that he could take lumber and start from scratch and build a new church. In 1999, the old church was torn down and the new facility was erected a short distance from the original church. We now worship in the new church. Rev. Michael Chapman retired in 2005.

Rev. Lillie Robinson came to Walker Chapel with expectations in 2005. She believed that there is nothing too hard for God. She would say, "don't fuss, just pray." The The members of Walker Chapel believed that their pastor was led by the Holy Spirit. Under the leadership of Rev. Robinson the first Women's Conference was held.

Members donated clothes for a closet for the community and went to Dallas, Texas for a Christian Education Conference.

Pastor Robinson and members visited and fed the whole community a Christmas meal. The pews were completely paid out. Programs were held to raise money for the mortgage each month. Pastor Lillie Robinson's favorite scripture was Psalm 91:1. "He that dwelleth in the secret place of the Most High shall abide under the shadow of the Almighty".

Rev. Quinton Hicks became the next Pastor of Walker Chapel A.M.E. Zion Church. He was outstanding and ready to do the work of the Lord. On Sunday, he was always early for church. Rev. Hicks preached hard. It didn't matter if the church was full or not. He would say, "stay in your own lane, and do the work God has assigned you to do." Rev. Hicks believed in the Book of Discipline of the A.M.E. Zion Church.

Presently, the Pastor of Walker Chapel A.M.E. Zion Church is Rev. Isabel Scott. She is not like others, she is different. She walked in with a smile and said she was Pastor Isabel Scott. She was totally ready to get about her Father's business. Rev. Scott has compassion for all of her sheep. She is a good Shepherd, wife and mother. She does all she can to encourage everybody to take an active part in church. We all work together. Walker Chapel loves the sermons Pastor Scott preaches (ex. Praise is your Weapon). We have our struggles, but we are still going on by the grace of God.

Rev. Scott is stronger than she has ever been. She says she never would have made it without the help of the Good Lord. Ride on King Jesus, the devil can not hinder me. She believes in prayer, fasting, praising and worshipping God. Her favorite Scripture is, "O taste and see that the Lord is Good!" Psalm 34:8.

Rev. Scott is blessed to have the Daughter of the House, Rev. Paula Essix, working beside her in the ministry. She is faithful, talented and a great help to us.

We thank those who have worked faithfully (past and present) beside the Pastors of Walker Chapel A.M.E. Zion Church to accomplish the great task of providing a place to worship and labors in the ministry.

PASTORS OF WALKER CHAPEL A.M.E. ZION CHURCH

Rev. Lalley

Rev. Wooten

Rev. Ghoston

Rev. S. S. Brunner

Rev. Spearman

Rev. Mable Kendrick

Rev. C. C. Craig

Rev. J. P. Phillips

Rev. Burt

Rev. J. P. Phillips

Rev. Dr. Floyd Chambers

Rev. Rebecca Gross

Rev. Clifton Granger

Rev. Michael Chapman

Rev. Lillie Robinson

Rev. Quniton Hicks

Rev. Isabel Scott

Bro. Ed (Chief) Walker was Preacher-Steward

of Walker Chapel for over 50 years

Maurine Hudson

Mamie Walker

Ozella Hockett

THE HISTORY OF
ST. PAUL AME ZION CHURCH-1875-2013
Pastor: Rev. Sylvester Turner
181 Wright Road
Cooksville, Mississippi

The first light that was shed on the minds of the group of organizers of this church has spread a beacon in the center of the hill that beckons men and women into its path.

It's a pleasure to look back over many years of human efforts, as in the year of 1875, when the late Elder W. M. Murphy was the founder, Elder E. D. Blancher was Pastor. We salute the efforts of the pioneers, who, without doubt, put God in front, and in spite of small financial gain, were able to hold on and push forward to now.

There is small doubt that a full history of St. Paul will ever be told for sealed eternally are lips of her early leaders who in many cases were not gifted in writing, or because of circumstances, they were unable to open their thoughts and deeds to posterity.

There wasn't much fashion, but much devoutness, there weren't lights but the Bible gave light for the way. The only warmth was a wooden heater, the warmth of God's love, and the love they had for each other. The records shows there were times St. Paul was in debt and the doors were about to be closed, but by prayers, the church held on.

The record shows that between 1875 and 1920, there have been approximately forty-five pastors and eight presiding elders. In the year of 1913 to 1917, there were three hundred members and fourteen class leaders. In 1917, the statistics of the church were written again. It stated that due to the migration period of southern blacks to the north, east, and west, the community and the church were badly affected and as a result, our membership was reduced to less than a half at that time.

In 1950's and 1960's, St. Paul suffered another loss; many members moved away and death over took many, which reduced the membership and the class leaders to six.

Since 1970 to 2013, there have been nine pastors and five presiding elders. Presently, we have twelve members and a wonderful Pastor, Elder Sylvester Turner.

"On Christ the solid rock we stand, All other ground is sinking sand."

St. Paul A.M.E. Zion Church
Cooksville, Mississippi
Elder Sylvester Turner, Pastor
Nevada Williams, Secretary

LIFT EVERY VOICE AND SING

(The Negro National Anthem: by: James Weldon Johnson)

Lift every voice and sing, till earth and heaven rings,
rings with the harmony of liberty. Let our rejoicing rise,
high as the listening skies; let it resound, loud as the roaring seas.
Sing a song, full of the faith that the dark past has taught us.
Sing a song, full o f the hope that the present has brought us.
Facing the rising sun, of a new day begun, let us march on, till victory is won.

Stony the road we trod, bitter the chastening rod,
felt from the days when hope unborn had died;
Yet with a steady beat, have not our weary feet,
come to the place, for which our fathers sighed.
We have come, over the way that with tears have been watered,
We have come, treading the path of the blood of the slaughtered,
Out from the gloomy past, till now we stand at last,
where the white gleam, of the bright star is cast.

God of our weary years, God of our silent tears,
Thou who hast brought us safe thus far on our way;
Thou who hast by thy might, led us into the light,
Keep us forever in the path, we pray.
lest our feet, stray from the pathway our God where we first met Thee.
Lest our hearts, drunk with the wine of the world, we forget thee;
Shadowed beneath Thy Hand, may we forever stand,
true to our God, true to our native land.

Chapter IV
GOD'S 21ST-CENTURY FREEDOM FIGHTER
Annie Devine

One of God's twenty-first century Freedom Fighters was chosen out of the Freedom Church, the African Methodist Episcopal Zion Church, namely, St. Paul of the City of Canton, Mississippi. God did not fail to bring The Freedom Church to the forefront of the Movement.

Activist Annie Devine gained national acclaim as a Challenger in the 1964 Mississippi Challenge. The Challenge confronted the seating of the regular Democratic Party from the State of Mississippi, which was all White, male, and was necessitated because the regular Party did not represent all the Citizens from Mississippi, namely, Blacks. The Challenge brought worldwide attention to the economic, political and social plight of African Americans in America and especially those living in the most dire, and oppressive conditions in the southern states. The passing of the Voting Rights Act of 1964 and the Civil Rights Acts of 1965 granted African Americans the right to vote without intimidation, discrimination, harassment and brutality, and enforced constitutional rights for African Americans and all disenfranchised citizens of this country.

The results of the Civil Rights Movement of the 60's was equal opportunities and political inclusion for Blacks and all disinfranchised people of all races in the United States. Black people could have a piece of the American Pie by putting people in political positions who would look out for their interests. The Civil Rights Movement hastened the day in which an African American, Barack Obama, could be elected president of the United States of America.

Activist Annie Devine was a gifted community organizer and God used her gifts in the organization of numerous programs to address the needs of people in Community Development, Medicine, Social Services, and Industry.

She is the recipient of numerous awards, citations and accolades of which some are: Mississippi Council of Human Relations and the National Committee for Independent Political Action. She was inducted into the

Voting Rights Hall of Fame, Selma Alabama, and Received an Honorary Doctorate Degree in Human Letters from Tougaloo College.

Being quick to share her knowledge and experience of the Civil rights Movement, she is quoted and referenced in many books and periodicals of which some are: *Coming of Age in Mississippi*, by Anne Moody, *Southern Journey* and *Freedom Ways* by Tom Dent, *Freedom is a Constant Struggle* and *Facts on Black Women in America* edited by: Darlene Clark Hine. She is also featured in several Documentaries including "Standing on my Sisters Shoulders and, Eyes on the Prize".

A lifelong member of St. Paul A.M.E. Zion Church, Canton, Mississippi, and a faithful witness for Jesus Christ. She served in various capacities, including: church secretary, choir member and president of senior choir, class leader, Sunday school teacher, conference worker, trustee and District Director of Christian Education.

She was raised by an aunt, Sally Sherrod, who was also a member of St. Paul and her uncle Alex Sherrod, who also pastored St. Paul and in the South Mississippi Conference.

As a child, she lived in the section of town called "Frog town", and remembers that at age about six Rev. McMullin pastored St. Paul. She was married to Andrew Devine and the mother of four children; Monette, Andrew, Barbara and Alex. She is the mother of Rev. Barbara Devine Russell, associate minister at St. Paul.

Her favorite Bible Scripture was Isaiah 54. To God be the Glory.

"Yet they are thy people and thine inheritance which Thou broughtest out by thy mighty power, and by thou stretched out hand".

Chapter V
AUXILIARIES

Auxiliaries are built into the history of the African Methodist Episcopal Zion Church, and have been supporting walls and the catalyst for effective Evangelism, Missionary work at home and abroad, Christian Education, Benevolence and Charitable endeavors, and for a unified, effective Laity.

The following Auxiliaries are major Ministries that have operated in the South Mississippi Conference since its inception:

WOMEN'S HOME AND OVERSEAS MISSIONARY SOCIETY (WH&OM)

CHRISTIAN EDUCATION

LAY COUNCIL

CONFERENCE WORKERS

WOMEN'S HOME AND OVERSEAS MISSIONARY SOCIETY:
(WH&OM)

The purpose of the Women's Home and Overseas Missionary Society of the African Methodist Episcopal Zion Church is:

<u>TO PROMOTE</u> growth in the knowledge and understanding of God and His Plan of redemption for the whole world, as revealed through Jesus Christ and the power of the Holy Spirit;

<u>TEACH</u> concepts of Christian Missions and provide experiences for participation in mission work and its ministries.

<u>EXEMPLIFY</u> the principles of Christian living and to win others to Christ.

<u>PROMOTE</u> the cause of World Evangelism, and serve as a financial support system to undergird the World Mission Outreach of the African Methodist Episcopal Zion Church, at home and overseas, to the end that, through the power of the Holy Spirit, Christ is exalted and God is glorified.

The WH&OM is spearheaded by the Episcopal Supervisor. The Districts are lead by Presidents, able missionaries in the South Mississippi Conference.

OFFICERS:

Missionary Supervisor
Mrs. Gwendolyn Brumfield

DISTRICT PRESIDENTS

CANTON-SHARON	JACKSON-GALLMAN	CANTON-PANOLA
Mrs. Monica Gilkey	Sis. Lidia Fisher	Mrs. Tesha Thompson
	COORDINATOR OF YAMS	
Mrs. Deborah Brown	Mrs. Bobbie Chambers	

SECRETARY OF YOUTH

Mrs. Darlene White   Ms. Katina Bell

SECRETARY OF YOUNG WOMEN

Mrs. Sandra Stanton

SUPERINTENDENT OF BUDS

Mrs. Patricia Glover   Sis. Heidi Eva Jones   Ms. Ashley Collins

SUPPLY CAPTAIN

Mrs. Shirley Brown   Mrs. Shirley Hampton   Ms. Citikita Brooks

President of Prayer Breakfast

LIFE MEMBERS COUNCIL

Sis. Annie Pearl Nichols   Mrs. Portia Jenkins   Mrs. Jacqueline Thompson

HEALTH COORDINATOR

Mrs. Angelina Brown   Ms. Stephanie Fisher   Ms. Vickie Harmon

MISSION EDUCATION DIRECTOR

Mrs. Bettye J. Nichols   Mrs. Emma Townsey   Ms. Glenetta Baker

The Mission of the WH&OM is the Great Commission*:*

All power is given unto me in heaven and in earth. Go ye therefore and teach all nations, baptizing them in the name of the Father and of the Son and of the Holy Ghost, teaching them to observe all things whatsoever I have commanded you, and lo, I am with you always, even unto the end of the world.

Matthew 28:18-20

THROW OUT THE LIFELINE,
THROW OUT THE LIFELINE,
SOMEONE IS DRIFTING AWAY,
THROW OUT THE LIFELINE,
THROW OUT THE LIFELINE,
SOMEONE IS SINKING TODAY.

PILLOWS OF THE WH&OM
South Mississippi Conference

Mrs. Blanche Horton Nichols from the Canton Jackson District under the leadership of Presiding Elder Jimmie C. Hicks, was honored at a Missionary Retirement Banquet at the Annual Conference of 1995 at Blair Metropolitan A.M.E. Zion Church, Jackson Mississippi.

Mrs. Nichols united with St. Paul A.M.E. Zion Church, Canton, Mississippi in 1936 after marrying Will Samuel Nichols and moving from the Middleton Grove A.M.E. Zion Church and Community. She has given her best in the service of the Lord at all times. She served as District President of WH&OM for twenty-seven years until she retired in 1996. She remained active in St. Paul Church until she was no longer able to attend. Mrs. Nichols was lovingly referred to as "Granny" by all the members in the South Mississippi Conference.

Her sense of humor was famous and she could make you 'laugh till you cried'. Granny's favorite saying was "give God His dime and obey Him, and you can live as long as you want." and she never failed to remind us that "Only What You Do For Christ Will Last."

Mrs. Theola Fluka, (picture not available) served as District President of the WH&OM for seventeen years on the Meridian Kosciusko District under the leadership of Presiding Elder Bennie Luckett, was honored along with Mrs. Blanche Nichols, at the Retirement Banquet at the Annual Conference of 1996 at Blair Metropolitan A.M.E. Zion Church by the Meridian-Kosciusko District. Mrs. Fluka was a member and faithful servant of St. Peter A.M.E. Zion Church in Meridian, Mississippi.

CHRISTIAN EDUCATION

The Christian Education Department is spearheaded by Conference Director, Mrs. Hattie Chambers:

(front Row: left-right: Rev. Dr. Mary Sims-Johnson, Ava Swinson, Episcopal Coordinator, CE, Rev. Acquanette Johnson, Bishop Mildred B. Hines, Clara Steele, Gladys Hughes, Rev. Dr. Belinda Johnson, second row: Carla Perry Johnson, Rev. Bonnie Travis, Quantae Walker, Latisha Johnson, Hattie Chambers, Ms. Horton, Lydia Johnson, Helen Parker, Camiel Brown, Edward Jean Blackmon; rear: Rev. Dr. Floyd E. Chambers & Rev. Gary D. Adams, Sr.

The South Mississippi Conference Christian Education Department Overview by Conference President, Hattie Chambers

The Christian Education Department (CED) of the African Methodist Episcopal Zion Church was founded in 1887.

The South Mississippi Conference is in compliance with the Zion Church to provide supervision, guidance, direction, and programmatic support for Christian training and nurture of children, youth, young adults and adults.

The South Mississippi Conference consists of three districts**: Canton-Panola, Canton-Sharon and Jackson-Gallman.**

It is our objective and mission to offer workshops, seminars, conferences and conventions which will help develop effective skills in Christian Educators and those striving for a closer walk with the Lord.

We also establish curriculums and seek various strategies to support Christian Education programs at every age level of the church. The Christian Education Department of the South Mississippi Conference strives to adhere to the Zion Book of Discipline.

DISTRICT DIRECTORS:

Jackson-Gallman	Jackson- Sharon	Canton-Panola
Lidia Fisher	Gladys Hughes	David O. Jones

PILLOWS OF CHRISTIAN EDUCATION IN THE
South Mississippi Conference:

Mrs. Dannie B. Jones (lt): A member of Zion Chapel A.M.E. Zion Church and school teacher in the Canton Public School District. She served on the Canton Jackson District as Director of Christian Education and served faithfully until her health failed her. She also served a number of years as a Consultant for the Christian Education Department

Mrs. **Mazalene Towner (rt):** A Christian Educator and a respected school teacher in the Canton Public School District. She was a member of the Zion Chapel A.M.E. Zion Church. She served as District Director of Christian Education on the Meridian-Kosciusko District faithfully until her death. A Scholarship Fund has been established in her honor and name to assist needy students who desire to attend college.

"Stand Up....Stand up....for Jesus

Christian Endeavor Pledge

"Trusting in the Lord Jesus Christ for strength, I promise Him that I will strive to do whatever He would like to have me do; that I will make it the rule of my life to pray and to read the Bible every day, and to support the work and worship of my own church in every way possible; and that just so far as I know how, throughout my whole life, I will endeavor to lead a Christian life."

LAY COUNCIL

The first Connectional Layman's organization of the African Methodist Episcopal Zion Church was established at the 1916 General Conference and the organization of the Lay members Association was adopted on May 18, 1916.

The purpose was to encourage spiritual growth and denominational loyalty and give the laity a voice, representation, and to insure proper consideration in the polity of the church.

The Laity is most visible in the electoral college from which members are elected delegates to the General Conference to represent the laity in the election of the Bishops.

The organization has been struggling to survive with the membership fluctuating due to lack of interest.

In 2008 Mr. Bruce Brown was appointed Conference president by Bishop Darryl B. Starnes and has served faithfully. According to President Bruce Brown, the South Mississippi Conference Lay Council has experienced fluctuating growth. Membership has peaked at 1300 and experienced a low of about 300. Presently the Lay Council has about 700 members. He is anticipating continuing growth in the laity both spiritually and numerically.

PILLOW OF THE LAY COUNCIL IN THE SMC

Mr. Ambrose Simpson, of Greater Blair Street A.M.E. Zion Church served faithfully and worked tirelessly in the 1970's and early 80's traveling extensively throughout the South Mississippi Conference, to raise awareness and organize a Lay Council in each church. After his death, his widow, Mrs. Mary Lynn Simpson took the helmet as District Director and worked tirelessly along with Conference President, Raymond Richmond, to build a viable organization. Mr. Raymond Richmond served faithfully until his health failed.

CONFERENCE WORKERS

The Conference Workers spearheaded by **Rev. Barbara Devine Russell (photo)**,was organized in 1841, the year of the first Annual Conference, by Mary Roberts. Zion Methodism was in its Infancy. Originally called, the Daughters of the Conference, this organization is replete with self-sacrifice and devotion to the cause of missions and the promulgation of the Gospel of Jesus Christ.

It is the second oldest benevolent organization, rivaled only by the Mother Society or the Missionary Society. The Missions operation was in their infancy, and the cry came from New York, New England, New Jersey and Pennsylvania; "send us the gospel, send a Minister, we need a Church." Thus, the great need was money to aid the Ministers in going to their mission fields to establish churches.

God, seeing the need of preachers out on the Missions Fields, placed a burning desire in the heart of Mary Roberts, to "do something" For these struggling Men of God. She began to organize programs to raise funds to send to the Ministers to sustain them as they built Zion Churches on this new frontier. Ms. Roberts' cause was not popular because the funds raised were being sent out of the local church, but she persevered against all odds, and her cause prevailed.

Mary Roberts' efforts helped spread the Gospel rapidly throughout the entire United States.

The Conference Workers have had a fluctuating ministry in the South Mississippi Conference. After lying dormant for a good many years, it was resurrected in 1996 when Bishop Joseph Johnson appointed Ms. Barbara Devine Russell as President. of the Conference Workers. She spearheaded a Bicentennial project which produced a Booklet in observance of 1996 Bicentennial entitled ***200 years In Zion.***

Sally Adams

The Conference Workers primary fundraising activity consist of an Annual Hat Show which is held in May of each year. The Conference Workers, under the leadership of Rev. Barbara Devine-Russell was given the privilege of compiling and editing this current book entitled*: " The South Mississippi Conference, The History, The Heritage, Heritage Edition 2013, which consist of* **A Compilation of the History of the Churches in the South Mississippi Conference.**

Mission:
TO EDIFY the Body of Christ through study and application of the Gospel of Jesus Christ, Spiritual Growth and Development and propagation of the Gospel of Jesus Christ.
TO PROMOTE education, missions and denominational loyalty by the power of the Holy Ghost, in order to **PRESERVE,** cherish and enlarge our heritage in Christ's Great Legacy as Missions Builders in the Kingdom of God.

OFFICERS

CONFERENCE PRESIDENT
Rev. Barbara Devine Russell

DISTRICT DIRECTORS:

Canton-Sharon	Rev. Barbara Devine Russell
Jackson-Gallman	Ms. Edna Pendelton
Canton-Panola	Ms. Sallie Adams

Colors: **Navy Blue and Gold**

Motto: **"All for Christ"**

"*I Can do all things through Christ which strengthens me.*"
Philippians 4:13

HIGHLIGHTS

**FROM THE 123RD SESSION OF THE
ANNUAL CONFERENCE CONVENED
AT SHARON CHAPEL A.M.E. ZION
CHURCH, OCTOBER 23, 2013**

Retirement was held for Rev. Dr. Jimmie C. Hicks, the **Statesman of the S.M.C. and** Mrs. Eunice Hicks, at the Rose of Sharon Family Life Center, at Sharon Chapel A.M.E. Zion Church where Rev. Hicks has been pastoring for thirty-eight years. The Hicks are highly esteemed pillows in the South Mississippi Conference for their Godly example and sterling Christian leadership. The retirement banquet was held on the exact same date, twenty Seven years later, after Rev. Hicks, Rev. Chambers and Rev. Luckett established "Operation Helping Ourselves," the Annual Home Mission Banquet, which is held during Annual Conference. Funds raised at the Banquet, are used to assist struggling churches in the South Mississippi Conference needing financial assistance for assessments, repairs, etc.

Elder Hicks is also one of the initiators of **Holy Week Services** along with Rev. Dr. Floyd E. Chamber, marveled that God planned his retirement to that exact date of the establishment of the Annual Home Mission Banquet

Rev. Terrell Blue from the Oklahoma Conference received the charge as the new pastor of Sharon Chapel A.M.E. Zion Church. Rev. Blue is accompanied by wife Paula, who is also a minister, and two children.

Rev. Dr. Aurillia Jones-Smith was appointed pastor of Victory A.M.E. Zion Church following Rev. Roderick Briggs' resignation.

Sis. Connie Davis-Thornton resigned as conference secretary after serving an exemplary twenty-seven years. Rev. Ola Dixon, previous assistant secretary was elected the new secretary and Sis. Heidi Jones was elected assistant conference secretary.

Rev. Gwendolyn Hampton returned to the S.M.C. after being away ten years, of which she attended and graduated from Hood Theological Seminary and Livingstone College. Rev. Hampton also pastored St. Luke A.M.E. Zion Church for eight years.

In a special conference convened at St. Paul A.M.E. Zion Church in Canton, Mississippi December 2013, Bishop Mildred Hines made history by dividing the SMC. into three Presiding Elder Districts. This move was necessitated by the need for more efficiency in the conference and also to stimulate growth.

Bishop Hines appointed two Episcopal Administrators to assist her in Conference and Episcopal matters: Rev. Dr. Floyd E. Chambers, and Rev. Dr. John C. Evans, Jr.

Bishop Hines called for integrity in all levels of the ministry. She admonished pastors to be faithful to their spouses in marriage and gave them a deadline to "clean up their personal affairs."

Bishop Hines required all pastors to file income taxes. Those who would not or could not adhere to these guidelines would not be allowed to continue to pastor in the South Mississippi Conference.

The South Mississippi Conference adopted as it's official motto: EXPECT THE GREAT .

Rev. John C. Evans, Jr., was appointed official Prayer Warrior of the South Mississippi Conference.

Rev. Rosie Jackson received the appointment to pastor Greater Blair Street A.M.E. Zion Church.

Rev. Jimmie C. Cable was retired as pastor of Gallman Chapel A.M.E. Zion Church after serving a tenure of thirty years in the South Mississippi Conference.

Rev. Derrick Baldwin from the Oklahoma Conference was appointed as the new pastor of Gallman Chapel A.M.E. Zion Church.

During the Bishop's third check up meeting held at St. Paul A.M.E. Zion Church at 505 south Union Street, Canton, Mississippi on July 19, 2014, Bishop Mildred b. Hines made the following changes: The official quadrennial Theme Song entitled I'm a Mountain Mover, was introduced;

Rev. Quinton Hicks was assigned pastor of Greater Middleton Grove; Rev. Moses Thompson was assigned to pastor Gallman Chapel A.M.E. Zion Church and St. James A.M.E. Zion Church was placed in the hands of Presiding Elder Gary D. Adams.

CONCLUSION

The History of the South Mississippi Conference, **Heritage Edition,**

Establishes the fact that the South Mississippi Conference was built up by the efforts of Missionary Preachers that were sent from the Tennessee-Mississippi Conference into the southern portion of the State of Mississippi to establish missions. These preachers went out into uncharted, dangerous territory; where slaves were running for their lives, and being aided by the Underground Railroad.

Slavery had been abolished but not abandoned. The period of Reconstruction was ended, and even though laws were passed to protect the rights of the freed African Americans, they were now being overturned and new laws passed to re-in-slave the Negro. Jim Crow laws and the Black Code Laws, which established the fact that the "Negro had no rights that the white man had to honor or respect."

This era witnessed the rise of the Ku Klux Klan, a hate group designed to keep the Negro in his place through terrifying and savage acts of cruelty which included intimidation, murders, lynchings, and merciless attacks by dogs upon the run-away slave and others who were accused of rebelling against these unjust laws. But God was marching on. Harriett Tubman had established an underground railroad that aided many slaves to freedom in the northern states.

It was in such a climate that Missionary Preachers begin the work of evangelizing and establishing missions in the Southern-most part of Mississippi in the early 1800's. Our forefathers did a great work for the Lord and the fruits of their labors are evident in the South Mississippi Conference.

In the book, "**The Reality of the Black Church**", (Bishop William J. Walls), Grandison Simms, N. J. Adams, Rev. Scurlock and Rev. Fulford are indeed established as missionary preachers who were sent from the Tennessee-Mississippi Conference to establish missions in the southern portion of Mississippi. These missionary preachers were destitute, hungry, homeless, in a strange, dangerous and hostile land, with no modern accommodation. But they gathered under old oak trees, in bush harbors, and slave huts to organize missions and to proclaim liberty to all the oppressed and the Good News of the Gospel of Jesus Christ.

They worshipped and praised the God who had brought them out of darkness into the marvelous light of His Son, our Lord and Savior, Jesus Christ. The newly established churches encountered hardships, destructions of every kind; fires, floods, storms, lightening and collapse, and also those destroyed during the Civil War. But they continued to worship in basements, members' homes, funeral homes, church parsonages and tents. Many times members had no money to pay the preacher, so they would "pound the preacher" with a pound of meat, vegetables, meal, four, or butter – and, they survived, they persevered, empowered and impelled by the Holy Ghost.

The South Mississippi Conference is thankful to God for the struggle and hard times, because it was through these that the early pioneers experienced God in a true and living way. They were drawn closer to Him, their faith was strengthened and they were able to persevere through all the trials and hard times because they knew that "weeping would endure only for a night, but joy comes in the morning." There was a brighter day ahead." Thanks be to our Forefathers and Mothers that we do not have to face the dangers, hardships and afflictions they encountered.

God has blessed the South Mississippi Conference, spiritually, numerically, financially and with large, beautiful edifices in which to worship and praise God; family life centers, recreational facilities, and all the modern conveniences. God has been good.

We thank and praise God for those faithful Pioneers and Pillows who laid the foundation for our generation, and for the sacrifices they made that we are now enjoying. We honor them for their love and service to God and for their perseverance against all odds, to spread the Good News of the Gospel of Jesus Christ to an oppressed people and to a dying world. Mississippi was one of the most oppressive states in the south, one in which slavery was "the vilest that ever saw the sun". But God chose to lift the shackles of slavery and liberate the African American through faith in Jesus, and praise and worship to Him that is able to keep us from falling and to present us faultless before the throne of God. for he whom the Son has made free, is free indeed. This message of liberation is for the whole world.

As we view the past, we can evaluate our present and forge the future by catching the vision of our founding fathers and through faith, praise, worship, discipleship, evangelism and Christian Service, press on toward the mark that Jesus commanded :

And he came and spake unto them saying, All power is given unto me in heaven and in earth. Go ye therefore, and teach all nations; baptizing them in the name of the Father, and of the Son and of the Holy Ghost; teaching them to observe all things whatsoever I have commanded you, and lo, I am with you always, even unto the end of the world. Amen.

Matthew 28:18-20

Wherefore, seeing we are compassed about with so great a cloud of witnesses, let us lay aside every weight, and the sin which so easily beset us, and let us run with patience the race that is set before us; looking unto Jesus, the author and finisher of our faith; who for the joy that was set before Him endured the cross, despising the shame, and is set down at the right hand of the throne of God.

BLESS BE THE TIE THAT BINDS,

OUR HEARTS IN CHRISTIAN LOVE,

THE FELLOWSHIP OF KINDRED MINDS,

IS LIKE TO THAT ABOVE.

THE LORD BLESS YOU AND KEEP YOU,

THE LORD LIFT UP HIS COUNTENANCE UPON
YOU AND BE GRACIOUS UNTO YOU.

THE LORD CAUSE HIS FACE TO SHINE UPON
YOU, AND GIVE YOU PEACE.

WHEN ALL God children get together what a time, what a time, what a time!

PHOTO GALLERY

CONFERENCE AND DISTRICT

OBSERVANCES &

PROGRAMS

Mrs. Ellen Richmond, guest speaker, is penned by Mrs. Blanche Nichols at Missionary Convocation

Above: Annual Conference-South Mississippi Banquet: seated center; Bishop Rueben Speaks & left wearing turban is Mrs. Janie Speaks. Presiding Elder Jimmie C. Hicks, standing.

(left: Mrs. Blanche Nichols and Rev. Sarah Rivers at Missionary Convocation

Rev. Bennie Luckett (right) and Rev. Floyd Chambers, left

District African American History Month Program.
(Mrs. Blanche Nichols, upper left, white hat)

Bishop Alfred E. White & Home Mission Queen Ora Williams

Christian Education Conference Retreat-- Conference President Audrey Richmond (rear, right : 3rd from end Raymond Richmond rear right)

**Bishop Nathaniel Jarrett & Missionary Supervisor Estelle Jarrett
Missionary Candlelight ceremony**

SMC Missionary Candlelight Ceremony – Zion Chapel AME Zion Church

**Missionary Convocation – (Rev. Author Davis, front right; Rev. Aurillia
Jones-Smith, left) Mrs. Andrea Grant lights candle (bottom)**

Lt to right: rear: Dis. Pres. De Leslie Graham, Radell Luckett, Deloris Cable, District President Georgetta Black, Maggie Sims. Front: Left: Hattie Rimmer, & Barbara Russell, Conference President.

Deloris Cable, Radell Luckett, Maggie Sims, Barbara Russell & Hattie Rimmer

Organizational meeting

Breakfast meeting Nancy's

**CW's Celebrate Bicentennial - 200 years in Zion with Jesus.
(Left to right: Clara Steele, Deloris Cable, Hattie Rimmer, Sallie Adams, and Barbara Russell, President)**

**Leadership Convocation, Bishop Nathaniel & Missionary Supervisor Estelle Jarrett
Second row second & third from right**

**Christian Education Convention; Conference President Hattie Chambers, third from
Left, front row; Terwinda Banks, third from left, rear.**

**Bicentennial Celebration, Canton-Jackson District
(Rev. Bonnie Travis-upper middle; Mrs. Hattie Chambers, left**

**(front-center: Presiding Elder Jimmie C. & Mrs. Eunice Hicks; rear: Rev.
J. P. Phillips & Rev. Bonnie Travis; Church Children, right)**

South Mississippi Conference turns new leaf as 20th Century Pillows Presiding Elders Bennie Luckett and Jimmie C. Hicks retire.

**Presidng Elder Emeritus Rev. Bennie & Mrs. Marcell Luckett
Retirement celebration at Greater Murphy**

**Presiding Elder Emeritus Rev. Jimmie C. & Mrs. Eunice Hicks
Retirement celebration at the Rose of Sharon (Sharon Chapel)**

**Bishop Hines January 2014
Checkup meeting
At Greater Sims AME Zion Church
Host Pastor Rev. Dr. Peggy McKenny (left)**

Rev. Lelar Brooks Leads worship Leader

**2ⁿᵈ Check-up Meeting Held in April 2014 at
Greater Sims opens with high praise**

**Sis. Heidi Jones SMC official cheer leading squad,
waves pom-pom along with other worshippers**

Mrs. David O. Jones, left.

Rev. Dr. Peggy McKenny, host Pastor, renders opening Scripture reading
Rev. Dr. John C. Evans, Jr. left and Rev. Gary Adams, right

Left, rear: Rev. Sammy Brown; left front: Rev. Aurillia Jones-Smith; inside: Rev. Isabel Scott

**BISHOPS THAT HAVE SERVED IN THE
SOUTH MISSISSIPPI CONFERENCE**

Charles Calvin Petty

1888 - 1900

Benjamin Garland Shaw

1924 - 1951

John Bryan Small

1896 - 1905

Buford Franklin Gordon

1944 - 1952

John Wesley Alstork

1900 - 1920

James Clair Taylor

1948 - 1954

William Leonard Lee

1916 - 1924

Stephen Gill Spottswood

1952 - 1956

John Wesley Wood

1920 - 1940

Charles Eubank Tucker

1956 - 1972

**BISHOPS THAT HAVE SERVED IN THE
SOUTH MISSISSIPPI CONFERENCE**

Clinton Rueben Coleman

1972 - 1980

Nathaniel Jarrett

1996 - 2004

Ruben Lee Speaks

1980 - 1984

Louis Hunter

2004 - 2008

Alfred E. White

1984 - 1992

Darryl B. Starnes

2008 - 2012

Joseph Johnson

1992 - 1996

Mildred Hines

2012 - present

A Tribute to Bishop Mildred B. Hines

For the completion of this special *"History and Heritage Edition of the South Mississippi Conference"*, I extend a special thanks to Bishop Mildred B. Hines, for this special time and season.

Ecclesiastes 3, expounds of times and seasons, times for everything, and seasons for various activities, under the heavens. The same can be said for the years of 2012 through 2016. The South Mississippi Conference was highly favored with the assignment of the 98th Bishop elected to the A. M. E. Zion Church, Bishop Mildred B. Hines.

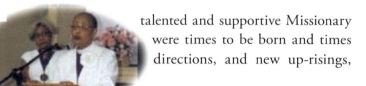

I thank her for this journey, for at her side is her talented and supportive Missionary Supervisor, Dr. Gwendolyn Brumfield. There were times to be born and times to die, they both brought new ideals, new directions, and new up-risings, while tearing down strong holds.

As a Bishop of humility, she offered times to plant and times to uproot and heal, appointing and reviving church leaders for better works. We witnessed times to tear down buildings and times to build new buildings and edifices. We were blessed with times to weep and an abundance of times to laugh, seldom times of mourning, yet many times to dance. For growth throughout the conference, she knew the time to scatter stones and the time to gather them.

During the many special gatherings, check-up meetings, annual conferences, we experience times to embrace and times to refrain from embracing, while serving this present age.

She stood strong as leaders expanded and retired, there came a time to search and a time to give up ties and relations. During constructive preaching and teaching, Bishop Hines provided precepts and concepts for times to keep and times to throw away, for ministries of kindness and better stewardship.

Thanks to Bishop Hines for allowing the Holy Spirit to lead her in such a mighty excursion. I thank her for superb leadership and love for the South Mississippi Conference. The History and Heritage of the South Mississippi Conference is comprised of beautiful edifices and *"God-Fearing"* leaders.

Resources:

"The African Methodist Episcopal Zion Church, Reality of the Black Church", William J. Walls

Scripture references are quoted from the New Living Translation and the King James Version of the Holy Bible

Church Historians:

Cathedral	Earnestine Davis (Consultant)
Free Union	Rev. Octavia Berry; Rev. G. L. Johnson
Free Chapel	Linda Thompson
Gallman Chapel	Edna Pendleton
Greater Blair Street	Rev. Rosie Jackson
Greater Middleton	Rev. Moses Thompson, Bruce Brown,
Grove	Christine Lee and Camiel Brown
Greater Murphy	Evelyn Mixon
Greater Salem	David O. Jones
Greater Sims Chapel	Willie C. Thomas, Sr.
Jerusalem Temple	Rev. Dr. Peggy McKenny, Ph.D. Theology
Lees Chapel	Quantae Walker
Liberty Hill	Rev. Acquanette Johnson
Owens Chapel	
St. James	Laurie M. Williams
	Virginia McCree
St. Paul – Canton	Rev. Barbara Devine Russell
St. Paul – Cooksville	Elder Sylvester Turner
	Nevada Williams, Secretary
St. Peter	Rev. Ola Dixon
Sharon chapel	Dr. Mary Sims-Johnson
Sharpsburg	Johnnie S. Brown
Tabernacle of Grace	Rev. Lillie Robinson

	Rev. Bessie Martin
Victory	Rev. Aurelia Jones-Smith
Walker Chapel	Rev. Paula Essix
Zion Chapel	Sallie Adams
Zion Hill	Laverne Monroe

Photos: Provided by:

Rev. Melvin Blackmon	Zion Hill AME Zion Church
Rev. Floyd Chambers	St. Paul, Canton & Zion Chapel
Mrs. Hattie Chambers	Zion Chapel
Rev. Acquannete Johnson	Liberty Hill AME Zion Church (CD)
Paula Essix	Walker Chapel AME Zion Church (CD)
Earl Nichols	St. Paul AME Zion Church, District picture
Rev. Barbara Devine Russell	

ABOUT THE AUTHOR

Barbara Devine Russell-Reed is a born again Christian, evangelist and minister of the Gospel of Jesus Christ.

She is a native Cantonian and a 1964 graduate of Rogers High School of which she graduated Historian of her class. She studied at several colleges and universities including Tougaloo Southern Christian College, Jackson State University, Jackson, Mississippi and Mott Community College in Flint Michigan. She is a 2013 graduate of New Foundation Theological Seminary where she received a degree in Christian Counseling.

She was formerly employed with the Genesee County Department of Veterans Affairs, Flint, Michigan; Mississippi Department of Public Welfare and the Mississippi Department of Corrections.

She is well known for her volunteer community services with at-risk children and youth, and voter registration and education outreach. Evangelist Reed is the daughter of the late nationally acclaimed Civil Rights Activist, Annie Devine. She is an Elder in the South Mississippi Annual Conference, and serves as assistant minister in her local church, St. Paul AME Zion Church, Canton, under the spiritual leadership of Rev. John C. Morris, Jr.

She is married to songwriter/musician Jerry Reed and they are the producers of a series of Gospel Meditations of which she is the featured vocalist. Evangelist Barbara is also a songwriter, gospel soloist and oratorical speaker.